T0360490

Cryptocurrencies

Already in just a decade of existence, cryptocurrencies have been the world's best-performing financial asset, outperforming stocks, bonds, commodities and currencies. This comprehensive, yet concise, book will enable the reader to learn about the nuts and bolts of cryptocurrencies, including their history, technology, regulations and economics. Additionally, this book teaches sound investment strategies that already work along with the spectrum of risks and returns.

This book provides a plain-language primer for beginners worldwide on how to confidently navigate the rapidly evolving world of cryptocurrencies. Beginning by cutting to the chase, the author lists the common burning questions about cryptocurrency and provides succinct answers. Next, he gives an overview of cryptocurrency's underlying technology: blockchain. He then explores the history of cryptocurrency and why it's attracted so much attention. With that foundation, readers will be ready to understand how to invest in cryptocurrency: how cryptocurrency differs from traditional investments, such as stocks; how to decide which cryptocurrency to invest in; how to acquire it; and how to send and receive it, along with investment strategies. Additionally, legal issues, social implications, cybersecurity risks and the vocabulary of cryptocurrency are also covered, including Bitcoin and the many alternative cryptocurrencies.

Written by a journalist-turned-professor, this book's appeal lies in its succinct, informative and easy-to-understand style. It will be of great interest to people looking to further their understanding of what cryptocurrency is, why it's a big deal, how to acquire it and how to send and receive it, as well as investment strategies.

Mark Grabowski is an associate professor at Adelphi University in New York where he teaches tech courses on Bitcoin and Blockchain, Internet Law, and Digital Ethics. Besides being an investor in cryptocurrency, he has advised cryptocurrency projects, been extensively quoted in the media on Bitcoin and blockchain and regularly speaks at international conferences on the legal issues surrounding cryptocurrency.

Routledge Focus on Economics and Finance

The fields of economics are constantly expanding and evolving. This growth presents challenges for readers trying to keep up with the latest important insights. Routledge Focus on Economics and Finance presents short books on the latest big topics, linking in with the most cutting-edge economics research.

Individually, each title in the series provides coverage of a key academic topic, whilst collectively the series forms a comprehensive collection across the whole spectrum of economics.

Reinventing Accounting and Finance Education
For a Caring, Inclusive and Sustainable Planet
Atul Shah

Microfinance
Research, Debates, Policy
Bernd Balkenhol

The Malaysian Banking Industry
Policies and Practices after the Asian Financial Crisis
Rozaimah Zainudin, Chan Sok Gee and Aidil Rizal Shahrin

Automation, Capitalism and the End of the Middle Class
Jon-Arild Johannessen

Cryptocurrencies
A Primer on Digital Money
Mark Grabowski

For a full list of titles in this series, please visit: www.routledge.com/
Routledge-Focus-on-Economics-and-Finance/book-series/RFEF

Cryptocurrencies
A Primer on Digital Money

Mark Grabowski

Routledge
Taylor & Francis Group

LONDON AND NEW YORK

First published 2019
by Routledge
2 Park Square, Milton Park, Abingdon, Oxon OX14 4RN

and by Routledge
52 Vanderbilt Avenue, New York, NY 10017

Routledge is an imprint of the Taylor & Francis Group, an informa business

British Library Cataloguing-in-Publication Data
A catalogue record for this book is available from the British Library

Library of Congress Cataloging-in-Publication Data
Names: Grabowski, Mark, author.
Title: Cryptocurrencies : a primer on digital money/Mark Grabowski.
Description: Abingdon, Oxon ; New York, NY : Routledge, 2019. | Series Routledge focus on economics and finance | Includes index.
Subjects: LCSH: Cryptocurrencies. | Digital money.
Classification: LCC HG1710 .G726 2019 | DDC 332.4—dc23
LC record available at https://lccn.loc.gov/2019013060

ISBN: 978-0-367-19267-9 (hbk)
ISBN: 978-0-429-20147-9 (ebk)

Typeset in Times New Roman
by Apex CoVantage, LLC

For my parents, Nancy and Ted Grabowski. It's impossible to thank you adequately for everything you've done for me.

Contents

Preface

Do you like learning about fascinating technology? Are you tired of wondering what the heck the blockchain is? Are you considering investing in Bitcoin, Ethereum, Ripple or some other cryptocurrency? Or maybe you'd just like to hold your own in a conversation on this topic with friends and coworkers?

My book is for beginners who wish to confidently navigate the rapidly evolving world of cryptocurrency. It covers how to invest in cryptocurrency and explains how it works and why it has become so popular.

I know what it's like to be in your shoes. When I first became curious about cryptocurrency, I had a lot of questions and doubts. Unfortunately, I quickly discovered that there really wasn't a one-stop resource, such as a book or video that explained everything I needed to know in simple language. I had to pore over hundreds of resources that were often convoluted in order to piece together explanations and grasp concepts. So, as a cryptocurrency investor and journalist-turned-professor, I decided to use my skills and experience to explain cryptocurrency in a succinct, informative and easy-to-understand way.

My book begins with an introduction that provides a brief overview of what cryptocurrency is and why it's important. That's followed by a list of frequently asked questions and brief answers. Next, I give a basic overview of cryptocurrency's underlying technology: blockchain. I then explore the history of cryptocurrency and why it's attracted so much attention. With that foundation, you will be ready to take on investing in cryptocurrency. You will learn how cryptocurrency differs from traditional investments, such as stocks; how to decide which cryptocurrency to invest in; how to acquire it; and how to send and receive it, along with investment strategies. Additionally, legal issues, cybersecurity risks and the vocabulary of cryptocurrency are also covered. As a final bonus: this book has a companion website, CryptocurrencyTextbook.com, which provides additional information, including instructional videos and useful links.

Thanks for reading!

Mark Grabowski

Author and Professor

Acknowledgments

Content from the following sources was reviewed as part of the author's research for this book. However, none of these sources have endorsed the book nor are they affiliated with the book or its author.

New York Times, CryptocurrencyFacts, Wikipedia, Quartz, the Foundation for the Defense of Democracies, Bitcoin.org, Parameter, Denis Zarytsky, Aziz Zainuddin, George Levy, Blockchain Institute of Technology, the Next Web, Digital Trends, Dash Force News, CoinDesk, *Cryptocurrency Investing Bible* by Alan T. Norman, CryptoCasey.com, F.S. Comeau, Ermos Kyriakides, Hacker Noon, CryptoMinded, Blockgeeks, Crush Crypto, Brave New Coin, CoinSutra, Coin Pupil, Thomas L. Smith, Warren Fauvel, the Motley Fool, Futurism, HistoryOfBitcoin.org, Crypto Daily, CryptoPotato, Master the Crypto, CCN, CoinCentral, Dustin Dreifuerst, *Blockchain for Dummies* by Manav Gupta, CNBC, Cointelegraph, *Wall Street Journal*, Digiconomist, HowMuch.net, CoinMarketCap, *Wired*, *TIME*, Smithsonian.com, *Bitcoin Magazine*, CryptoWatchDogs, *Washington Post*, Stanford University Computer Science Department, Eric Roberts, CryptoTimeline.com, Electronic Frontier Foundation, Gawker, Virgin Galactic, Princeton University, IMDb, *Forbes*, Bitsonline, Lifehacker, KGTV San Diego, Business Insider, *New York Post*, *The* (London) *Sun*, Peter Brandt, BrainStuff, *Esquire*, Ipsos, Finder.com, 99Bitcoins, Vitalik Buterin, Investopedia, TechRepublic, the Wrap, Charlie Bilello, Journographica, DeadCoins.com, Kryptovaluta Norge, Howtotoken, Crypto Coin News, POS Monkey, *Science*, Bitcoin Market Journal, BitcoinExchangeGuide.com, Law Technology Today, Max Ambrose, Coinbase, Chainanalysis, Messari, Premier Offshore Tax & Corporate Services, TechCrunch, CryptoSlate, HoweyCoins.com, *Financial Times*, Trustnodes, *Los Angeles Times*, Gallup, Satis Group, Finance Magnates, Bitcoin.com, *Harvard Business Review*, LendEDU, PricewaterhouseCoopers, Jason Bloomberg, Norbert Michel, Heritage Foundation, *Handbook of High Frequency Trading* by Greg Gregoriou, Satoshi Nakamoto, U.S. Commodity Futures Trading

Commission, U.S. Securities and Exchange Commission, Gab, Crypto Research Report, SwissBorg, Zach Stafford, Murad Mahmudov, U.S. Senator Thomas Carper, James Canton, Anthony Pompliano, Vice News, Simply Explained – Savjee, *Barron's*, *Glamour*, Alexia Bonatsos, University of Luxembourg, Southern Poverty Law Center, *Jerusalem Post*, Hackernoon, *Fortune*, Paul Merriman, MarketWatch, Hired.com, Glassdoor, LinkedIn, Student Loan Report, CUNY Crypto Club at Baruch College, Breaker, the Block, *Ledger Journal*, *Stanford Journal of Blockchain Law & Policy*, Invest in Blockchain, *The Spectator*, Nick Szabo, Andreas Antonopoulos, Library of Congress, Heritage Foundation, CoinSwitch, Axios, Coinmonks, Hassnain Javed, the Daily Hodl, Raconteur, *Bloomberg Businessweek*, Brad Barber, Crypto Briefing, Norton Cybersecurity, *Independent*, Foley & Lardner.

1 Introduction

U.S. Senator Thomas Carper astutely observed in 2013, "Virtual currencies, perhaps most notably Bitcoin, have captured the imagination of some, struck fear among others, and confused the heck out of the rest of us."[1]

Today, cryptocurrencies are arguably the hottest investment product currently available, but still somewhat of a geeky trend not understood by most people. And that is exactly why you should learn about it and consider investing in it. Jumping on the bandwagon earlier than most will give you an edge, both in terms of experience and potential profits. To wit, this book will help teach you the nuts and bolts of cryptocurrency, including its history, technology, regulations and economics. Most importantly, you'll learn sound investment strategies that already work along with the spectrum of risks and returns.

In short, cryptocurrency is basically a new form of digital money that is shifting the paradigm and challenging the legacy financial system.

> **Renowned digital currency expert Andreas Antonopoulos likens cryptocurrency to "the Internet of money."**

Ever since 2009, when a mysterious figure known as Satoshi Nakamoto invented Bitcoin and with it blockchain technology, cryptocurrency has grown into a global phenomenon. You'll have a hard time finding a major financial institution, a prominent tech company or a government that has not researched cryptocurrencies, published a paper about it or started a blockchain project. About half of the world's top-50 universities now offer at least one undergraduate course in cryptocurrencies. A 2018 study found that while only 9% of people worldwide owned cryptocurrency at the moment, the number investing was expected to almost triple in the near future.[2]

For a growing number of enthusiasts, cryptocurrency not only represents a once-in-a-generation wealth building opportunity but also has the potential to be part of an economic revolution. "It's a new form of thinking about money, storing money, transferring money, and just dealing, organizing, and understanding money, and all kinds of second order financial effects that come out of that," explained cryptocurrency analyst Murad Mahmudov.[3]

Renowned digital currency expert Andreas Antonopoulos likens cryptocurrency to "the Internet of money."[4] In the same way that the Internet flattened the communication structure and allowed anyone anywhere on earth to communicate, cryptocurrency can do that with money. Its blockchain technology allows anyone to instantly and securely engage with anyone in world economically without a bank account or middleman. Cryptocurrency also offers many upgrades over traditional money or fiat, such as the following:

- It's valuable. Unlike fiat, cryptocurrency such as Bitcoin can't be created out of thin air, and only a limited number will ever be produced, which makes it a scarce asset that's unlikely to depreciate.
- It's efficient. Cryptocurrency transactions are also faster, less costly and more secure than fiat transactions because they don't utilize a third party, such as a bank.
- It's uncensorable. Instead of being regulated by bureaucrats behind closed doors like government-backed currencies, cryptocurrency is regulated by mathematics and cryptography. There is no headquarters or central place for cryptocurrencies such as Bitcoin, which makes it nearly impossible to shut down and stop. Transactions are also more private.

These features, combined with its ability to be easily converted into traditional currencies, makes it a very attractive financial asset for citizens of any country and a necessity for those in turbulent developing nations. For example, when Turkey's lira fell 20% overnight in 2018 as the United States imposed sanctions, Turkish cryptocurrency exchange usage saw a massive spike, as Turkish citizens recognized that putting their money into cryptocurrency would help them avoid the lira's impending depreciation.

Although cryptocurrency is often purchased as a long-term investment, it can also be used as a medium for purchasing products and services – everything from pizza to flights. With so many use cases, it's no wonder the total daily value in money transferred by all cryptocurrency networks is comparable to the value transferred by Mastercard's network. The rise of cryptocurrencies represents "the legitimization of an emerging asset class alongside the traditional global economy," according to Dr. James Canton of the Institute for Global Futures.[5]

Cryptocurrency is not without its controversies, however. Terrorists, criminals and hate groups have all utilized cryptocurrency to evade authorities and fund their illicit activities. But it's also being increasingly utilized to do good and help people. For example, when Roya Mahboob launched a woman's rights blog in Afghanistan, she paid her female contributors in Bitcoin, as they did not have bank accounts. Meanwhile, the United Nations has used cryptocurrency to aid over 10,000 Syrian refugees.

Another drawback is that cryptocurrency has its financial risks. As with the dot-com boom, cryptocurrency has had its shares of ups and downs. Market volatility, scams, regulations and other setbacks have created uncertainty and doubt. Some individuals have lost their savings, spouses and even the will to live as a result of poor investment decisions.

But the bottom line is, cryptocurrency is likely here to stay and just getting started. For those in the developing world, it's a form of financial populism that takes power away from corrupt governments and central banks, and puts economic power in the hands of people. And for the rest of the world, it's a special investment opportunity. Those who get involved now and invest in the right opportunities may well reap the same bragging rights and riches as the early Internet pioneers who backed Amazon and Facebook. "This is still a nascent technology, it's only 10-years-old," said Anthony Pompliano, founder of Morgan Creek Capital Management. "But it's been the best-performing asset over the past 10 years. It's beaten stocks, bonds, commodities and currencies."[6]

The choice is yours: you can remain confused and hesitant, or you can read on and learn how to become part of history in the making.

Notes

1 Aruna Viswanatha, "U.S. Officials: Virtual Currencies Vulnerable to Money Laundering," *Reuters* (Nov. 18, 2013), available at www.reuters.com/article/us-senate-virtualcurrency/virtual-currencies-vulnerable-to-money-laundering-u-s-justice-idUSBRE9AH0P120131118.
2 Ana Alexandre, "ING Bank Survey Reveals Interest in Crypto Will Double in Near Future," *Cointelegraph* (June 27, 2018), available at https://cointelegraph.com/news/ing-bank-survey-reveals-interest-in-crypto-will-double-in-near-future.
3 Anthony Pompliano, "Murad Mahmudov: The Ultimate Bitcoin Argument," *Medium* (Oct. 31, 2018), available at https://medium.com/@apompliano/murad-mahmudov-the-ultimate-bitcoin-argument-b205a1987408.
4 Andreas M. Antonopoulos, *The Internet of Money*, Sheridan, Wyoming: Merkle Bloom (Aug. 30, 2016).
5 N.A., "10 Reasons Why Cryptocurrency Is the Next Big Thing," *CoinSwitch* (July 18, 2018), available at https://coinswitch.co/news/reasons-why-cryptocurrency-is-the-next-big-thing.
6 Anthony Pompliano, interview, *CNN* (Nov. 23, 2018), available at https://twitter.com/APompliano/status/1066058486851739648.

2 Frequently asked questions

Let's begin by cutting to the chase. Next are quick answers to common burning questions about cryptocurrency:

What's Bitcoin?

Bitcoin is a type of digital asset that can be bought, sold or transferred between parties over the Internet. Because of this, it's used to store value, like gold or real estate. It also serves as a form of digital money that can be used to purchase products and services, and to make payments to others over the Internet. Bitcoin is just one of hundreds of cryptocurrencies, but it's the first and most valuable one.

Isn't it fake money?

Bitcoin, along with all cryptocurrencies, only exists in cyberspace. There's no way to download your coins and physically hold them in your hands like traditional money. However, cryptocurrency can be exchanged fairly easily for real money, such as U.S. dollars, on exchanges such as Coinbase.com. Cryptocurrency can also be used to buy food, airline tickets and even cars. So, it has real-world value.

Who invented it?

Bitcoin, the first cryptocurrency, launched in 2009. It was created by Satoshi Nakamoto. This name is believed to be a pseudonym, and his true identity remains a mystery. He could be a she or a group of people. Nakamoto disappeared shortly after creating Bitcoin. His parting words in a 2011 email stated he had "moved on to other things."

Why is it such a big deal?

Some historians see cryptocurrency as the latest phase in the evolution of money. Many technologists are intrigued by the potential of its innovative blockchain technology. For numerous entrepreneurs, especially early adopters, cryptocurrency represents a once-in-a-generation wealth opportunity.

What's the point of cryptocurrency?

Cryptocurrency revolutionizes the way transactions are sent over the Internet. It's fast, secure, relatively anonymous and doesn't require a middleman, such as a bank, which reduces transaction costs and makes it censorship resistant. Thousands of merchants accept payment with Bitcoin – including Subway, Whole Foods, Microsoft, Overstock.com and several airlines.

How is cryptocurrency's price determined?

As with traditional investments, such as stocks, cryptocurrency's price is determined by the market – how much people are willing to pay for it. Because this market is still in its infancy, prices often fluctuate.

How do I buy cryptocurrency?

Numerous ways exist to invest in and buy cryptocurrency. I recommend using an American online cryptocurrency exchange, such as Coinbase.com. It's easy to buy and sell cryptocurrency on, very secure and has an excellent reputation.

Do you have to be rich to invest?

Although Bitcoin is quite expensive, with a single coin costing several thousand dollars, you don't need to be rich to invest in cryptocurrency. You don't have to buy a whole Bitcoin; you can buy a very small fraction of a Bitcoin. There are also hundreds of other cryptocurrencies you can invest in, and some cost less than a penny per coin.

I heard Bitcoin is only used by criminals.

Cryptocurrency is often stereotyped by the mainstream media as something that's only used by criminals for illegal activities, but a 2018 study by the Foundation for Defense of Democracies found that only 1% of all Bitcoin is used for illegal transactions.[1]

So, it's legal?

The U.S. government allows cryptocurrency, but you are required to pay taxes on your investment profits. However, a small number of countries, such as Pakistan, have banned cryptocurrency.

But isn't it risky?

Cryptocurrency is often likened to the Old Wild West. The market is highly volatile. Scams are prevalent. It's largely unregulated. It takes time, research and a certain personality to succeed. Fortunately, I've written this book to guide you.

What do experts think?

The world's financial bigwigs have mixed opinions on cryptocurrency. Some won't touch it with a 10-foot pole, while others believe it will do for financial transactions what Amazon did to e-commerce or what Facebook did to social media. Jamie Dimon, CEO of JPMorgan said, "It's a fraud." But James Gorman, CEO of Morgan Stanley, believes it's "more than just a fad." Nobel Prize winning economist Paul Krugman said, "Bitcoin is evil." On the other hand, Janet Yellen, chairwoman of the U.S. Federal Reserve, called it "a very important new technology." Warren Buffett, CEO of Berkshire Hathaway, cautioned that it's "a real bubble." Meanwhile, Christine Lagarde, managing director of the International Monetary Fund, predicted it "might just give existing currencies and monetary policy a run for their money."[2]

Notes

1 Yaya J. Fanusie and Tom Robinson, "Bitcoin Laundering: An Analysis of Illicit Flows into Digital Currency Services," *Foundation for Defense of Democracies* (Jan. 12, 2018), available at http://defenddemocracy.org/content/uploads/docu ments/MEMO_Bitcoin_Laundering.pdf.
2 Joon Ian Wong and John Detrixhe, "What the World's Financial Bigwigs Think about Bitcoin," *Quartz* (Sept. 29, 2017), available at https://qz.com/1089740/ what-the-worlds-financial-bigwigs-think-about-bitcoin/.

3   Fundamentals

You're probably eager to jump in and purchase your first Bitcoin so you can start making money. But before we get into investing, it's important for you to have an understanding of the fundamentals behind cryptocurrency – namely, its blockchain technology.

What's blockchain?

Think back to the last time you bought a brand name item, such as a handbag or a luxury watch. Or suppose you wanted to purchase a rare, expensive item, like an antique or a rare baseball card. How could you tell that it was genuine and not counterfeit or stolen? Having accurate records and a way to verify the authenticity of things we buy is essential. It requires reliable systems that are trustworthy and tamperproof. But in a world of fake news, Internet scams and hackers, how can we trust the information we receive?

Blockchain is an online bookkeeping platform or ledger that is incorruptible, enforces transparency and bypasses censorship.

The solution is in a technology known as blockchain, which can provide a single source of truth that's verifiable, secure and immutable. Blockchain is basically a ledger or collection of records. Ledgers are nothing new; they've been used in double-entry bookkeeping for hundreds of years. But blockchain offers an innovative upgrade. A crowd oversees and maintains records across a wide network of computers, rather than relying on a single entity, like a bank or government, which typically hosts data on a particular server. Because no individual controls blockchain records, they can't be as easily changed and are more secure. As records are added, they are grouped in a block that shows the chain of custody by linking them all the way back to their origin – hence, the term "blockchain." Blockchain utilizes military-grade cryptography to ensure records are permanent and can't be changed.

Relation to cryptocurrency

Blockchain is the technology behind cryptocurrencies such as Bitcoin (Figure 3.1), which is the first and best known use of blockchain. Cryptocurrency is a type of digital asset that can be bought, sold or transferred between parties over the Internet. Because of this, it's used to store value – much like gold, real estate and other types of traditional investments. As with other investments, its value is determined by the market – how much people are willing to pay for it. Cryptocurrency also serves as a form of digital currency that can be used to purchase products and services, and to make payments to others over the Internet.

However, it differs from traditional currency in many ways. Unlike U.S. dollars and euros, which can also be used electronically, there are no physical coins or paper bills for cryptocurrency. In addition, unlike traditional

Figure 3.1 This is a depiction of Bitcoin. There is no actual physical coin that's a Bitcoin. Cryptocurrency only exists in cyberspace – you can't hold it in your hand like a penny or dollar bill.

Source: Eivind Pedersen

money, cryptocurrencies are decentralized. When you send cryptocurrency to someone or use it to buy something, you don't need to use a bank, credit card or any other third-party intermediary to coordinate that transaction. The transaction goes directly from you to the other person and arrives securely and almost instantly – all without any middleman involved.

Transferring things online from one person directly to another is nothing new. Email and instant messaging, for example, are examples of peer-to-peer communication. You can send documents, photos and other types of files easily and instantly over the web. However, whenever you want to send money over the Internet, you need to enlist the services of a third party, such as a bank, a credit card or PayPal to ensure the transfer took place. You can't simply just attach money to an email and send it to someone like you would a photo. Otherwise, anyone could just make a copy of that money as they can with photos and documents. If digital money can be copied, it becomes worthless. There would be nothing to prevent copying it many times over and sharing it with multiple people. This issue is what's known as the double spend problem (Figure 3.2), and it's why we currently have a need for banks and other money transfer services to serve as middlemen in online transactions.

Cryptocurrency offers a solution to this problem through a special type of transparent, decentralized ledger technology known as blockchain. Cryptocurrency is encrypted in a way that prevents it from being copied. Every transaction involving the cryptocurrency is recorded onto a publicly viewable database – the blockchain. The transfer of cryptocurrency from one person to another is confirmed by a global network of computers that verify both that a person actually has ownership of the cryptocurrency that he

Figure 3.2 Illustration of the "double spend" problem

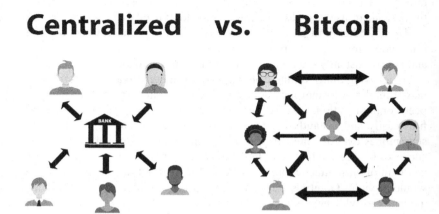

Figure 3.3 Illustration of centralized vs. decentralized networks

or she claims to have and that the person hasn't already spent it in a different transaction. So, instead of having a centralized database in which transactions are certified by a third party, such as a bank, cryptocurrency uses blockchain technology to securely verify, confirm and record each transaction.

Because the data is stored in a fully decentralized manner across a global network of computers instead of a centralized database, there's no single point of failure. This makes blockchain records more secure than banks and less vulnerable to fraud, tampering or a systemwide crash. And, best of all, with a decentralized blockchain (Figure 3.3), there's no middleman needed to arbitrate the transaction, dictate terms and take a big cut along the way. Unlike banks – which typically operate 9 to 5, charge fees for transactions, limit how much money you can withdraw from an ATM or wire to someone and sometimes take days to process deposits – cryptocurrency allows you to send and receive an unlimited amount 24-7 anywhere in the world at no cost.

How cryptocurrency works

You may wonder, how is this possible? How can you make transactions without an overarching system pulling the strings? In cryptocurrency, the traditional mediators who manage transactions like banks do are replaced by a network of computers owned by various people all over the world.

These computers use their processing power to verify, confirm and approve transactions. They're incentivized with cryptocurrency rewards to help manage the blockchain.

Although Bitcoin, and alternative cryptocurrencies, all utilize blockchain technology, they do so in differing ways. The most common methods are known as Proof of Work (PoW) and Proof of Stake (PoS).

Bitcoin uses a PoW system to process transactions. The system's software is free to download, and anyone can run it – it's what's known as a "permissionless" blockchain. However, it requires technical expertise, specialized hardware and lots of electricity. Those who run Bitcoin's software, known as miners, use their computers (known as "rigs"; Figure 3.4) to solve encrypted puzzles that verify the accuracy of the transactions. This encryption technology, known as SHA-256, was developed by the National Security Agency (NSA).

The first miner to solve these puzzles receives some of the currency, also known as a block reward. In Bitcoin, a new block challenge occurs every 10 minutes, and the winner receives 12.5 Bitcoins. Once the problem is solved, the transactions are grouped into a block of data that is added to the block-chain. The new block is publicly viewable and links all the way back to the initial transaction on the blockchain known as the Genesis block.

Figure 3.4 Bitcoin mining rig
Source: http://rebcenter-moscow.ru/

Manav Gupta, author of *Blockchain for Dummies*, explains how this process makes the blockchain so secure:

> Each block contains a hash (a digital fingerprint or unique identifier), timestamped batches of recent transactions, and the hash of the previous block. The previous block hash links the blocks together and prevents any block from being altered or a block being inserted between two existing blocks. In this way, each subsequent block strengthens the verification of the previous block and hence the entire blockchain. The method renders the blockchain tamper-evident, lending to the key attribute of immutability.[1]

Copies of the ever-growing blockchain are stored on another set of computers known as "nodes," which are voluntarily operated. Because nodes, unlike miners, receive no compensation, they are typically operated by people who are invested in Bitcoin and therefore want to see it succeed. In order to mine, a person must also run a node or be part of a mining group that operates a node.

Having thousands of mining computers around the world compete against each other to solve the same problem for a winner-takes-all prize can be inefficient, however. Bitcoin is often criticized by environmentalists for all the energy it wastes. Consequently, many newer cryptocurrencies utilize the more environmentally friendly PoS approach to verify transactions. Under this system, only those who own the cryptocurrency can verify transactions. Those who manage PoS systems are known as forgers. The more of a cryptocurrency they own, the more rewards they can collect for verifying transactions on their computers, which are known as masternodes. Like mining, forging requires technical expertise and special software. Plus, you need to buy a considerable amount of coins to be eligible to forge. In other words, mining and forging are not something that's easy to take up for the casual cryptocurrency investor.

Some blockchains use a hybrid that seeks to combine the best elements of PoW and PoS known as Proof of Activity (PoA). PoW, PoS and PoA are all based on consensus, meaning that a majority of the network must approve transactions. If one node generates a different output than others, an algorithm known as Byzantine fault tolerance is used to settle disputes among network participants. Once confirmed, transactions cannot be modified or removed. Because of these features, it is virtually impossible to hack cryptocurrencies to create false transactions or mint new coins. For example, if someone helping to maintain the database of all Bitcoin transactions changed his own copy of the records to add more Bitcoins to his account, the other computers maintaining the records would see the discrepancy, and the changes would be ignored. This design helps ensure honesty in an anonymous and trustless environment.

In order to tamper with the blockchain, a single person would need to control a majority of the network, which is known as a 51% attack. Decentralizing the network across thousands of computers and participants helps ensure no one individual becomes that powerful. Not to mention, it would be a very costly endeavor to gain that much control.

If you're not a miner, you can only get cryptocurrency from someone who already has it. As with traditional money, cryptocurrency can be earned as payment (for example, some tech companies pay employees in Bitcoin and thousands of merchants accept it), purchased on exchanges or gifted. Of course, you could also acquire cryptocurrency by creating your own cryptocurrency. Many entrepreneurs have gotten rich that way. But doing so requires technical knowledge or enough money to hire a savvy developer. And that's not even the hardest part. Launching a successful cryptocurrency also requires giving it a useful purpose, building the infrastructure, maintaining it and convincing others to buy it.

Once you've acquired cryptocurrency, you'll be able to generate a private key, which enables you to digitally sign off on all transactions. The key is a long string of randomly generated letters and numbers that are virtually impossible to crack thanks to a strong encryption code base. You can only lose your cryptocurrency if you forget your private key or if someone else knows it and uses it to steal your cryptocurrency. When sending cryptocurrency, you will be identified only by an alphanumeric identity, known as a public key, thus providing pseudonymity. Your real identity can only be revealed if someone knows the public key associated with your name. Thus you need not worry about your personal data being shared with third parties. However, if you acquire cryptocurrency on an exchange that follows Know Your Customer (KYC) guidelines, you can be sure that the government can track down all of your transactions on the blockchain.

Other applications

Cryptocurrencies like Bitcoin are just one type of crypto asset. Other digital assets utilize blockchain to regulate the creation of new units, verify transactions and secure the transactions without the intervention of any middleman. For example, blockchain is also used for cryptocollectibles such as "CryptoKitties," a popular app that enables users to purchase, raise and breed unique virtual pets. By 2018, the app had attracted more than 200,000 users and generated over $50 million in transactions.[2] Securities such as stocks, bonds and equities are also beginning to make their way to the blockchain, allowing for direct and secure peer-to-peer transactions without a financial intermediary. Eventually, many traditional assets could be digitized and accounted for using the blockchain.

Besides making transactions, blockchain can also be used to set up agreements or contracts of sorts. For example, if you wanted to buy or rent property, you could do it through a decentralized blockchain and avoid using banks and real estate brokers – and their costly middlemen fees. You could pay the home seller or landlord in cryptocurrency. In turn, you'd receive the home deed or digital entry key, which would arrive by a specified date. If the key didn't come on time, the blockchain would release a refund. If the other party sent the key before the rental date, the function would hold it until you paid and the date arrived. The blockchain would record the transaction and provide a receipt you can view online. Disintermediated agreements such as this are known as "smart contracts."

Blockchain can also be used in many industries where financial exchanges aren't necessary in transactions. Although Bitcoin is "permissionless" and public, meaning anyone can participate in its network and view its ledger, that's not the only way a blockchain can be built. A blockchain can be built that requires permission to view its information, that limits which parties can make transactions and that sets who can serve as nodes that validate transactions. (It should be noted, however, that some blockchain purists don't consider such restricted ledgers to be a bona fide blockchain.)

In health care, patients' records could be encoded and stored on the blockchain with a private key that would grant access only to specific doctors. This could help ensure that medical privacy laws aren't violated. Another potential application for blockchain is elections. Instead of lining up at polling stations, showing ID and completing forms, voting could be done securely online. The convenience might help bolster turnout, especially among young people. And because blockchain is more secure than traditional record keeping, it could help allay concerns about foreign governments hacking elections. Blockchain could also be used to build a social network that can offer features existing platforms don't. With Facebook, Twitter, Tumblr and other social media giants facing increasing criticism for restricting certain speech and even banning users, a decentralized social media platform that's censorship resistant could someday emerge as an alternative.

Blockchain is shaking up more than just money and is already being utilized by many Fortune 500 companies. Walmart, Amazon and Apple have had a lot of success using blockchain technology to track products. In July 2018, IBM landed a $740 million contract to help implement blockchain tech in Australia's government. The company now employs approximately 1,500 blockchain-specific staff members. According to Pricewaterhouse-Coopers's 2018 Global Blockchain Survey, 84% of executives surveyed said their companies are "actively involved" with the technology.[3] If the bubble bursts on the cryptocurrency market, it seems likely that at least the underlying blockchain technology will thrive. As the *Wall Street Journal*'s Christopher Mims predicted in a March 11, 2018, story, "Blockchain will survive, even if Bitcoin doesn't. . . . [The] latest blockchain applications could bring overdue change to critical, if unsexy, functions in shipping, real estate and . . . diamonds."[4]

Limitations

But some experts warn that the hype about blockchain is just that. Although cryptocurrency has experienced tremendous growth since its beginning in 2009, it suffered through a recession in 2018. This may be attributed in part to cautious investors who are holding back funds until cryptocurrency delivers on its promise. Enthusiasm over blockchain by the corporate world has also slipped as a result. A November 2018 analysis by Axios found that corporate executives were dropping blockchain buzzwords much less on earnings calls and during presentations to analysts and investors.[5] "The blockchain revolution will have to wait a little longer," predicted Martha Bennett, principal analyst for Forrester Research.[6] Cryptocurrency and its blockchain technology both need to make a number of improvements before becoming entrenched deeply into society. Let's cover some of the biggest weaknesses holding it back.

Complexity: First of all, blockchain technology is complex. The use of technical computing terms can confuse and deter outsiders. So, it requires some focused time and energy to wrap your head around. Not everyone is willing to put in that effort. While there are a plethora of websites and books available to explain it, a 2018 study by personal finance website Finder found that nearly one-third of Americans find cryptocurrency too difficult to understand.[7] Many mainstream media journalists have also been criticized for failing to grasp and explain the topic to the public, as well.

Speculative markets: Traditional investments like stocks and bonds are well developed, regulated and fairly stable. Cryptocurrency is not. However, due to the potentially disruptive nature of it, people have taken to speculating on the value of the digital economy it might create. Because cryptocurrency markets are still in their infancy and don't operate like traditional investments, they are prone to rapid fluctuation and manipulation. While this can create large rewards, it also presents high degrees of uncertainty for cryptocurrency.

Decentralization: Decentralization is one of the biggest advantages of cryptocurrency, but it's also one of its biggest weaknesses. When the

U.S. stock market or dollar struggles, the government can attempt to correct it by adjusting interest rates or making tax cuts. By contrast, the cryptocurrency market is highly volatile – perhaps even manipulated by a handful of big investors or "whales" – and can't easily be corrected. For example, after hitting an all-time high value of nearly $20,000 in December 2017, Bitcoin's value declined sharply to about $6,000 by July 2018. It rebounded above $8,000, but in November 2018 dropped below $4,000.

Irreversibility: To prevent double spending, a transaction can't be reversed. By anyone. Not you, not your bank, not police, not Bitcoin's inventor. No one can help you. If something goes wrong with a transaction and cryptocurrency is lost in cyberspace, there is no way to recover it. If a hacker steals cryptocurrency from an online exchange or if you forget your private key, you won't be able to recover the funds. Scams are rampant, and there's no safety net to protect you.

Wasteful: Cryptocurrency networks require a staggering amount of energy to operate. According to a 2017 report by Digiconomist, the amount of energy used annually to mine Bitcoin alone could power three million households in the United States. While Bitcoin offers many advantages over traditional means of transaction, it requires 60 times the amount of energy that Visa uses for the many more credit card transactions it processes each year.[8]

Speed: Blockchain networks require nodes to operate. But as many cryptocurrencies are new, their networks lack enough nodes to facilitate widespread usage. Backlogs of transactions often build up. Consequently, many networks now charge transaction fees to provide incentives to people to utilize their computers to serve as nodes. Transactions are often prioritized by the amount of fees people are willing to pay to send cryptocurrency, creating a supply and demand scenario. Thus, you get what you pay for. The less you're willing to pay, the longer your transaction will take. That said, the speed of cryptocurrency transactions is improving rapidly. Visa still has the fastest transaction speeds over any other payment network, with 24,000 transactions per second. The fastest cryptocurrency is Nano, which can process about 7,000 transactions per second (and does so free of charge), making it faster than PayPal's 193 transactions per second. Bitcoin, however, processes a measly seven transactions per second.[9]

Legal uncertainty: Given all these aforementioned issues, regulation rumors have begun to heat up as countries around the world grapple with how to treat cryptocurrency. Some seem welcoming while others are downright antagonistic. Pakistan, for example, has banned cryptocurrency. The United States, at the time of this writing, has no clear cryptocurrency policy other than taxing profits made on investments and a few other regulations. But U.S. officials have said that more regulations are needed. Given that cryptocurrency was created to circumvent the government, it's no surprise that investors tend to react badly to even the mere suggestion of new laws. Cryptocurrency's 2018 recession initially began due to rumors that a ban would be imposed by South Korea, one of the top-five countries for cryptocurrency.

As you can see, cryptocurrency right now is more of a great concept than a perfected product. But keep in mind that cryptocurrency is still in the very early stages. Visa was founded in 1958 and has had 60 years to improve and grow its capabilities. If we give cryptocurrency some more time to develop its technology, many of these issues may be fixed. For example, many cryptocurrency developers are attempting to implement sharding, which would make a blockchain faster and more energy efficient.

Sharding involves partitioning a blockchain so that each node would have only a part of the database instead of the entire information. It's considered a scaling solution for blockchains because, as they grow larger, network performance begins to slow if every node is required to carry the full blockchain. Currently, several blockchain projects are working on implementing sharding in cryptocurrency. Some popular projects include Zilliqa and Cardano. Whichever project can successfully do this first will likely become very lucrative.

Despite these obstacles, Forrester's Bennett is optimistic about the future of blockchain: "To quote Amara's Law: 'We tend to overestimate the effect of a technology in the short run and underestimate the effect in the long run.'"[10]

Notes

1 Manav Gupta, *Blockchain for Dummies*, Wiley (2018), available at www-01. ibm.com/common/ssi/cgi-bin/ssialias?htmlfid=XIM12354USEN.
2 Alex Tapscott, "Cryptocurrency Is Just One of Seven Types of Cryptoassets You Should Know," *Quartz* (July 25, 2018), available at https://qz.com/1335481/ cryptocurrency-is-just-one-of-seven-types-of-cryptoassets-you-should-know/.
3 Steve Davies and Grainne McNamara, "PwC's Global Blockchain Survey 2018," *PricewaterhouseCoopers* (Aug. 2018), available at www.pwc.com/gx/ en/issues/blockchain/blockchain-in-business.html.
4 Christopher Mims, "Why Blockchain Will Survive, Even If Bitcoin Doesn't," *Wall Street Journal* (Mar. 11, 2018), available at www.wsj.com/articles/why-blockchain-will-survive-even-if-bitcoin-doesnt-1520769600.

5 Courtenay Brown, "Corporate America's Blockchain and Bitcoin Fever Is over," *Axios* (Nov. 11, 2018), available at www.axios.com/corporate-america-blockchain-bitcoin-fervor-over-fb13bc5c-81fd-4c12-8a7b-07ad107817ca.html.

6 Martha Bennett, "Predictions 2018: The Blockchain Revolution Will Have to Wait a Little Longer," *Forrester* (Nov. 9, 2017), available at https://go.forrester.com/blogs/predictions-2018-the-blockchain-revolution-will-have-to-wait-a-little-longer/.

7 N.A., "Why Haven't We All Bought Cryptocurrency Yet?" *Finder* (Feb. 2018), available at https://go.forrester.com/blogs/predictions-2018-the-blockchain-revolution-will-have-to-wait-a-little-longer/.

8 N.A., "Bitcoin Energy Consumption Index," *Digiconomist* (2018), available at https://digiconomist.net/bitcoin-energy-consumption.

9 Daniel O'Keeffe, "Understanding Cryptocurrency Transaction Speeds," *Coinmonks* (June 5, 2018), available at https://medium.com/coinmonks/understanding-cryptocurrency-transaction-speeds-f9731fd93cb3.

10 See supra note 6 (Bennett).

4 History

Cryptocurrency, such as Bitcoin, has become all the rage. Some historians see it as the latest phase in the evolution of money. Many technologists are intrigued by the potential of its innovative blockchain technology. For numerous entrepreneurs, especially early adopters, cryptocurrency represents a once-in-a-generation wealth opportunity. However, it's also suffered numerous cybercrimes and market crashes, resulting in a chorus of critics warning that it's risky and perhaps a pyramid scheme.

To understand how we got to this point and what all the excitement and controversy are about, let's take a look at the history of cryptocurrency.

Cryptocurrency is the latest attempt to reinvent the way we exchange money. Throughout history, humans have relied on some sort of payment system to purchase goods and services. People initially used a bartering system, swapping things like livestock for grain. But this proved to be a difficult and inconsistent way to determine value. To remedy the inconvenience of bartering, intermediaries such as gold were used as a medium of exchange. Unfortunately, precious metals have a limited supply because they are difficult to produce. Thus, gold and silver were eventually replaced by government-issued currencies or fiat, such as the U.S. dollar and the euro. But because it's easy to make a lot of paper money, fiat faces debasement and inflation.

If there has been one consistent theme regarding the evolution of payments, it's that people prefer payments that are convenient and transactional. Consequently, some economists and historians consider cryptocurrency the most important payment invention since gold. Bitcoin began the cryptocurrency revolution when it launched in 2009. But it had several earlier ancestors and developments that made it possible.

1970s–1980s: origins

The origin of cryptocurrency is, of course, related to the beginning of the Internet, which revolutionized the world like nothing before. After all, if there was no global system of interconnected computer networks, crypto-currency wouldn't be able to function.

The first ever transaction over the Internet allegedly occurred back in 1972, when the Internet was known as ARPANET and only used by military officials and academic researchers. Stanford University and MIT students struck a deal to sell and buy some weed. However, as the Smithsonian notes, "This exchange doesn't check all the boxes for e-commerce: it was illegal and money wasn't transferred online. Instead, the event probably represents the first deal facilitated by the Internet."[1] But it illustrated the transactional possibilities for the Internet.

A 1976 paper by Stanford engineering professor Martin Hellman and his research assistant Whitfield Diffie described some of the technology that would later help make online transactions possible. Nearly 40 years later, the pair was recognized for their groundbreaking contribution, winning the 2015 Turing Award, widely considered the most prestigious award in the field of computer science. Other researchers who developed key technologies between the late 1970s and early 1980s that later helped make cryptocurrency possible include Ralph Merkle, a computer science professor at Georgia Tech; Neal Koblitz, a math professor at the University of Washington; Victor Miller, a math professor at the University of Massachusetts–Boston; and Leslie Lamport, a computer scientist at Microsoft.

In 1983, a research paper by then-UC Berkeley graduate student David Chaum (Figure 4.1) introduced the idea of untraceable digital cash. "You can pay for access to a database, buy software or a newsletter by email, play a computer game over the net, receive $5 owed you by a friend, or just order a pizza," he explained at a conference. "The possibilities are truly unlimited."[2]

Chaum is sometimes called the godfather of anonymous communication because he invented many cryptographic protocols that laid the groundwork for cryptocurrency. He was a pioneer in the so-called cypherpunk movement, which believed that privacy was necessary for an open society in the Internet Age, but that government, corporations and other faceless organizations couldn't be counted on to provide it. Therefore, it was necessary to create and encourage widespread use of strong cryptography and privacy-enhancing technologies as a route to social and political change. "You have to let your readers know how important this is," Chaum told a *Wired* journalist.

Cyberspace doesn't have all the physical constraints. . . . There are no walls . . . it's a different, scary, weird place, and with identification it's

Figure 4.1 David Chaum speaking at TTI/Vanguard
Source: Asa Mathat

a panopticon nightmare. Right? Everything you do could be known to anyone else, could be recorded forever. It's antithetical to the basic principle underlying the mechanisms of democracy.[3]

Chaum's ideology would help inspire the creation of Bitcoin decades later. Unfortunately, his ideas were way ahead of his time and struggled to gain adoption. DigiCash, the company Chaum founded in 1989 to make his vision a reality, declared bankruptcy, and he abandoned the project.

Initially, there was great reluctance to utilize the Internet for transactions. Banks and merchants were deterred by technical difficulties and legal uncertainties. The first true e-commerce transaction didn't happen until the early 1990s, when online merchants began listing products on the World Wide Web and accepting credit cards. No one knows exactly for sure what that first transaction was – like many things in history, it depends on who you ask. But soon after, e-commerce began to take off. In 1994, Stanford Federal Credit Union in Silicon Valley became the first bank to offer online banking services to all of its members. Amazon launched the same year. It is now the world's third most valuable company and accounts for 43% of all online sales.

1990s: dot-com boom

In the mid-1990s, the dot-com boom began and with it came the first working digital currencies. One of the first was E-gold, founded in 1996 and backed by gold. It was unique compared to traditional payment methods in that it was purely digital in nature and transactions were completely irreversible. It became hugely popular and had more than five million users. Although E-gold was likely started with benevolent intentions, it quickly became a haven for criminals and was subsequently shut down by the U.S. government.

Silicon Valley entrepreneurs looked for new ways to improve online transactions. A major breakthrough came in 1998 when Elon Musk, Peter Thiel and others founded PayPal. The worldwide online payment system supports money transfers over the Internet and serves as a digital alternative to traditional paper methods like checks and money orders. PayPal remains to this day a very popular and successful way of sending money in cyberspace, although it now faces growing competition from Google Wallets and Apple Pay.

While both E-gold and PayPal helped facilitate online transactions, they lacked many of the characteristics of cryptocurrency. For one thing, both represent a claim of value: E-gold was a digital representation of gold and PayPal was a digital transfer of fiat. A cryptocurrency, by contrast, is a value itself. Additionally, both E-gold and PayPal were managed by a central authority coordinating transactions. Cryptocurrencies, on the other hand, are decentralized, meaning there's no middleman that coordinates transactions between two parties. Still, E-gold and PayPal were important precursors to Bitcoin because they demonstrated the ability to utilize cyberspace to transfer funds and make purchases.

Around the same time that these online payment systems launched, a group of NSA researchers published a paper in a law journal that outlined a system very much like Bitcoin in which secure financial transactions were possible through the use of a decentralized network. In 1998, two computer scientists took this concept a step further. Nick Szabo designed a decentralized digital currency he called "Bit Gold." Szabo proposed using "smart contracts," which are digital contracts that cut out the middleman using computer supervision. He later worked with Bitcoin's founder to help Bitcoin get off the ground.

Meanwhile, Wei Dai outlined the basic properties of all modern-day cryptocurrency systems in a paper entitled "B-Money, an Anonymous, Distributed Electronic Cash System." Neither Bit Gold nor b-money were ever implemented, but they are widely regarded as direct precursors to Bitcoin's architecture. In fact, Dai's work was cited in Bitcoin's proposal. As a tribute to Wei Dai's contribution, the smallest unit of a now popular cryptocurrency known as Ethereum is called the wei.

Legendary economists such as Milton Friedman agreed that the concept of cryptocurrency was a brilliant idea whose time had finally come. "The one thing that's missing, but that will soon be developed, is a reliable e-cash, a method whereby on the Internet you can transfer funds from A to B, without A knowing B or B knowing A," the Nobel Laureate said in a 1999 interview.[4] However, it would be another decade before the idea for cryptocurrency became a reality.

2008: Bitcoin's birth

Enter Bitcoin. Although Bitcoin isn't the first proposed cryptocurrency, it's notable because it is the first working cryptocurrency. Equally important is the trailblazing, record-keeping technology it introduced to the world: blockchain.

Bitcoin's history begins on Halloween in 2008. October 31 was the day that Satoshi Nakamoto published his white paper, which outlined his vision for this new currency and technology. Nakamoto proposed "a purely peer-to-peer version of electronic cash that would allow online payments to be sent directly from one party to another without going through a financial institution."[5] Only eight-pages long and distributed for free online, this white paper began the whole cryptocurrency and blockchain movement.

The launch of Bitcoin occurred in the midst of the global financial crisis of 2008. That's probably not a coincidence. The public had become very distrustful of the government and big banks to manage their money, opening the door to a new way of doing things.

Nakamoto offered a forward-thinking way to change long-established financial protocols. Using Bitcoin, funds could potentially be transferred anywhere in the world instantly, anonymously and without middleman fees or government oversight. "Until Satoshi emerged out of nowhere . . . nobody believed it was even possible," explained Hassnain Javed, a columnist for *The Nation*. "Satoshi proved it was."[6] Patrick McDaniel, a computer science professor at Penn State University, called Bitcoin "an intellectual artifact. It's the frontier of economics."[7] He wasn't the only one enamored. Many and varied successful people took notice and wanted in. Morgan Stanley CEO James Gorman, Federal Reserve Chairwoman Janet Yellen, Vice President Al Gore, BlackRock CEO Larry Fink, businessman Mark Cuban, actor Ashton Kutcher, rapper Nas and world champion boxer Mike Tyson have all extolled the virtues of cryptocurrency. Nakamoto's fame spread so far that he was even nominated for the Nobel Prize in Economics in 2015.

> **Bitcoin's founder remains an unsolved mystery.**

You may be wondering, who is this visionary, and where did he come from? This is where the history of cryptocurrency turns into something of a mystery novel. Nakamoto completely disappeared shortly after launching Bitcoin. No one really knows who Bitcoin's founder is. The name Satoshi Nakamoto is believed to be a pseudonym, and his identity remains a mystery. He could be a she or group of people. Although there have been many rumors, claims and debates about who is Nakamoto, his identity has never been adequately verified. Adding to the mystery, Nakamoto has not accessed his Bitcoin wallet, which contains over one million Bitcoins, placing its value in the billions of dollars.

Before vanishing, Nakamoto appointed a successor: Gavin Andresen, a software developer who helped build Bitcoin's original code. Nakamoto's parting words in an email stated, "I've moved on to other things. It's in good hands with Gavin and everyone."[8] Andresen later founded a nonprofit organization called the Bitcoin Foundation to help further develop and publicize Bitcoin. In homage to Nakamoto, the smallest fraction of a Bitcoin that can be sent (which is currently a hundredth of a millionth of one Bitcoin) is known as a satoshi.

Bitcoin came to life on January 3, 2009. That's the date of the so-called Genesis block, or the first block of transactions published on the Bitcoin blockchain. The first block also includes text from Nakamoto noting the failure of traditional banking. Cryptocurrency was no longer just an idea. Nakamoto's dream was now a reality. But it took time to turn the fledgling technology into a robust, anonymous, decentralized payment system.

Initially, Bitcoin had no monetary value. Its computer software was available free online, and programmers would acquire Bitcoin through a process known commonly as "Proof of Work" or mining, which involves the solving of difficult cryptographic problems using computers. Miners would trade Bitcoin back and forth for fun. Hal Finney, a video game developer from California, is credited with being the first miner of Bitcoin and the first to receive a transaction from Nakamoto.

The first theoretical price for Bitcoin was established October 5, 2009, when New Liberty Standard published an exchange rate it calculated by measuring the cost of electricity for a computer to generate a Bitcoin through mining. That rate was a fraction of a penny. Now it costs thousands of dollars and requires powerful computers to mine one Bitcoin because so many people are doing it. If miners are making Bitcoin too fast, the system algorithmically throttles creation of coins, of which only 21 million will ever be made. Because of this slow, predictable rate of growth, Bitcoin is far more likely to deflate, meaning it will increase in value over time unlike traditional fiat currencies.

"What makes the likes of Bitcoin extraordinary is that the currency is limited in quantity, thus functioning more like precious metals," explains journalist Lionel Shriver.

> Producing a single Bitcoin requires so much computing power that environmentalists have criticized the process as cataclysmically wasteful of energy. Further, every Bitcoin mined requires more computing power than the one before, meaning that the total coinage in circulation rapidly approaches an absolute mathematical limit.[9]

2010: Bitcoin pizza day

Soon after its exchange rate was established, Bitcoins could be purchased in addition to being earned through mining. In February 2010, BitcoinMarket.com was created by a programmer known only by the online handle of "dwdollar." This is widely believed to be the first exchange that sold Bitcoin (and first cryptocurrency exchange, for that matter). It was a brilliant initiative, but it was ahead of its time. The exchange struggled to gain traction, experienced financial issues and soon folded.

Bitcoin encountered another setback later in 2010 when a major vulnerability in its code was spotted. Transactions weren't properly verified before they were included in the blockchain, which let users bypass Bitcoin's restrictions and create an unlimited number of Bitcoins. Fortunately, within hours, the bug was spotted and fixed. This is the only known major security flaw found and exploited in Bitcoin's history.

Despite these early growing pains, Bitcoin had a bright future ahead.

The first thing ever bought with Bitcoin was pizza.

May 22, 2010, marked Bitcoin's first retail purchase. It was the first time anyone had actually used Bitcoin to purchase any kind of good or product. As such, it's a very notable date in cryptocurrency history, and it's often colloquially referred to as Bitcoin Pizza Day.

A Florida programmer named Laszlo Hanyecz posted on a Bitcoin forum that he was interested in buying pizzas with Bitcoins. He negotiated to get $25 worth of pizza – two pizzas delivered by Papa John's – in exchange for 10,000 of his Bitcoins. When you work out the numbers, that transaction pegged the price of Bitcoin to a quarter of a penny. So, that means that he had to pay four Bitcoin for every penny worth of that pizza. That transaction essentially established the initial real-world price or value of Bitcoin. And it showed that Bitcoin could actually be used as a means of payment.

Soon after, new Bitcoin exchanges, such as MtGox and Tradehill, opened. Over a five-day period beginning on July 12, the market value of Bitcoin increased ten times from less than a penny to eight cents. By November 2010, Bitcoin's marketcap reached $1 million, and Bitcoin's price reached 50 cents per coin. The first mobile transaction occurred in December 2010.

2011: Silk Road and altcoins

The use of Bitcoin to make purchases really took off in January 2011 when a website known as Silk Road (Figure 4.2) was established. It served as an online marketplace for selling illicit drugs, and it accepted Bitcoin. This helped Bitcoin get going because all of a sudden, it had a real use case. Because cryptocurrency can be sent by anyone to anyone with relative anonymity, the digital rights group Electronic Frontier Foundation dubbed it "a censorship-resistant digital currency."[10] Consequently, WikiLeaks began accepting Bitcoin when the U.S. government pressured traditional payment processors such as Visa and Mastercard to block donations. Soon, a critical mass of people were using Bitcoin to fund all kinds of secret and sordid transactions. By February 2011, Bitcoin reached parity with the U.S. dollar, selling at a rate of one Bitcoin for one dollar.

Unfortunately, Bitcoin's association with unlawful sites tainted its reputation. Despite Silk Road ultimately being shut down by law enforcement

Silk Road
anonymous marketplace

Welcome **nique!**
messages(0) | orders(0) | account(฿0) | settings | log out
🛒(0)

Shop by category:
Cannabis(137)
Ecstasy(18)
Psychedelics(77)
Opioids(38)
Stimulants(60)
Dissociatives(7)
Other(106)
Benzos(42)

1 hit of LSD
(blotter)
฿1.64

1/8 oz high
quality cannabis
฿4.12

1 g pure MDMA
(white)
฿4.90

Step-by-step:
1. Get anonymous money
2. Buy something here
3. Enjoy it when it arrives!

back to **business as usual**

recent feedback:

seller	rating	feedback	
edgarnumbers(100)	5 of 5	Excellent packaging. The pill was left entirely intact. Not crushed one bit. Would definitely buy again!	item
dexsource	5 of 5	Product arrived well protected and on time, no complaints.	item
Goldismoney(97)	5 of 5	Top quality! Would use again!	item
3Jane(99)	5 of 5	Fast and discreet.	item
crimson(100)	5 of 5	legit. you do pay for quality service.	item
psynom(100)	5 of 5	Good communication, quick delivery. I didnt test the product yet, but it looks good.	item
easypeezy	5 of 5	Fast shipping. Gave some freebies. Highly recommended!	item
Ivory(100)	5 of 5	tasty stuff. packaging could have been a little less stinky	item
swch	5 of 5	Good Swiss Quality (strong) weed. All went as agreed, very good and legit seller, thanks!	item
kaliforniaProducts(100)	5 of 5	Outstanding product but get a vacuum sealer	item

฿1 = $15.64

become a seller | how does it work? | community forums | contact us

Figure 4.2 Screenshot of the now defunct Silk Road

Source: Dr. Monica Barratt

and many legitimate businesses now accepting Bitcoin, to this day, Bitcoin is often stigmatized in the media as a currency that only criminals use to buy and sell illegal things.

But publicity is publicity as they say. And this saying certainly proved true for Bitcoin. Following an article published by Gawker about Silk Road and Bitcoin, Bitcoin's price skyrocketed. "If it catches on," *Time* magazine predicted in an April 2011 story, "Bitcoin might pose a threat not just to governments, but to payment processors as well."[11] Bitcoin hit almost $30 in June 2011 before falling and ending 2011 valued at just over $5. Thus began a trend in price volatility, which remains present to this day.

Bitcoin's increasing media coverage and rising price began to catch the attention of other tech entrepreneurs, who saw the potential to make money from cryptocurrency. For the first couple years of its existence, Bitcoin had been synonymous with cryptocurrency because it was the only cryptocurrency.

It wasn't until 2011 that other competitors appeared, such as Litecoin. These alternative coins, or "altcoins" as they're often called, were forks of Bitcoin using its open-source code and were intended to improve upon certain elements of the Bitcoin design, such as speed or anonymity. There are presently thousands of cryptocurrencies, but Bitcoin remains by far the leading one in terms of recognition and marketcap.

2012–2016: growth and setbacks

The next five years brought about major growth for cryptocurrency coupled with several significant setbacks.

In 2012, WordPress became the first notable online merchant to accept payment in Bitcoin, and it was soon followed by other major retailers, such as Microsoft. This was considered the first step toward cryptocurrency being widely accepted as a legitimate payment method. It created a "network effect." As UC Berkeley economics professor Hal Varian explained,

> Just as a fax machine is valuable to you only if lots of other people you correspond with also have fax machines, a currency is valuable to you only if a lot of people you transact with are willing to accept it as payment.[12]

Bitcoin also became part of pop culture. Popular network TV shows such as CBS's *The Good Wife* featured a storyline involving Bitcoin.

Despite these positive developments, Bitcoin's price remained volatile, hitting $15 in August 2012 but then dropping to $7 two days later. Adding to concerns, Bitcoin was drawing criticisms from environmentalists about the amount of energy its network used to process transactions. In response, two programmers, Sunny King and Scott Nadal, proposed using a new method, known as Proof of Stake, to reduce the processing power and electricity necessary to manage cryptocurrency transactions. Many cryptocurrencies developed since then utilize this more environmentally friendly method.

In 2013, entrepreneur JR Willet introduced a new initiative to the cryptocurrency market known as the initial coin offering or ICO. The ICO is a means of crowdfunding a blockchain start-up via a presale on its forthcoming cryptocurrency. The first coin to utilize an ICO was Mastercoin. Soon, many projects were utilizing ICOs, but it proved to be controversial because many ICOs did not have a working product. They were nothing more than an idea. And there wasn't any regulatory oversight placed on them. As a result, ICOs became exploited by scammers who would take investors' money and disappear without ever launching. A 2018 study found that investors lost money in as many as 80% of ICOs.[13] Consequently, many nations now ban ICOs completely.

Bitcoin has also encountered some legal obstacles. In March of 2013, the U.S. government began imposing restrictions on U.S.-based cryptocurrency exchanges, requiring them to register as money services businesses and comply with money laundering laws. In June 2013, the Bitcoin Foundation received a letter from the California Department of Financial Institutions requesting that it "cease and desist from conducting the business of money transmission in this state."[14] But in November 2013, the foundation's lawyer testified before a U.S. Senate committee and federal lawmakers were generally positive about Bitcoin. Cryptocurrency remained legal to own and transfer in the United States, despite some state officials' objections. But other countries were less welcoming. Thailand banned Bitcoin that same year, and more nations would follow. The threat of regulation gave pause to potential institutional investors. "Bitcoin is a technological tour de force," Google Chairman Eric Schmidt told CNBC in a 2013 interview. "What I don't know is, ultimately, is it going to be legal?"[15]

Despite these legal challenges and all the new competing projects generated by ICO funding, Bitcoin continued to be king of the cryptocurrency market in 2013. Adoption of Bitcoin widened. Richard Branson's Virgin Galactic began accepting Bitcoin for space travel. He observed, "It feels strange to think of a world without cash, no more coins or notes to find down the back of the sofa, but it appears that's the way things are heading."[16] On May 2, 2013, the world's first Bitcoin ATM opened in San Diego, California. There are now thousands of cryptocurrency ATMs worldwide. On November 28, 2013, Bitcoin passed the $1,000 mark per coin. This was quite remarkable; that one Bitcoin that was worth a quarter of a penny four years earlier was now worth $1,100! Bitcoin's marketcap had surpassed $1 billion, and its network was moving more money than Western Union.

Wall Street and U.S. government officials began paying more attention to cryptocurrency. A Bitcoin ticker was added to the Bloomberg terminal so that Bitcoin's value could be tracked in real time. "It is clear that Bitcoin can be used as money," a U.S. court opined in a ruling, adding, "It can be used to purchase goods or services."[17] Federal Reserve Chairman Ben Bernanke said virtual currencies "may hold long-term promise, particularly if the innovations promote a faster, more secure and more efficient payment system."[18]

In 2014, PayPal started accepting Bitcoin payments for merchants. Popular online retailer Overstock.com also began accepting Bitcoin. The Federal Election Commission approved Bitcoin donations to politicians. The European Union began regulating cryptocurrencies. No longer was Bitcoin something just used by techies and cypherpunks. The cryptocurrency market was beginning to attract many retail investors. Exchanges began flourishing.

The most popular by far was MtGox. The Japan-based exchange was originally launched in 2006 by American programmer Jed McCaleb, an Arkansas native who dropped out of UC Berkeley. He initially created MtGox as a marketplace for people to trade cards for an online fantasy game known as "Magic: The Gathering Online." That venture didn't make much money, however, so in July 2010, McCaleb converted it into a Bitcoin exchange. It was an ingenious pivot. MtGox was the first Bitcoin exchange that really gained traction and took off. A year later, McCaleb sold the website to a

Frenchman living in Japan. McCaleb remained involved in cryptocurrency, working on popular projects, such as Stellar and Ripple, and is now one of the richest people in the world.

Unfortunately, MtGox struggled after the change of ownership. In February 2014, the exchange was hacked, resulting in account holders collectively losing nearly a million Bitcoins. The entire cryptocurrency market suffered. Bitcoin's price dropped to about $300 per coin. The scandal illustrates the costly risks involved with cryptocurrency and why critics sometimes liken it to the Old Wild West.

Despite these risks, interest in cryptocurrency continued to grow. Cryptocurrency news site CoinDesk hosted Consensus, the first of what would become a popular annual cryptocurrency conference in New York City. No longer were cryptocurrency enthusiasts having small meetings in a Silicon Valley living room or coffee shop; conferences like Consensus were attracting thousands of participants from around the world and cryptocurrency news sites like CoinDesk were getting millions of views.

Adoption continued, too. There were now an estimated 160,000 merchants accepting Bitcoin. Prominent venture capitalists and entrepreneurs began entering the market. The New York Stock Exchange invested $75 million in Coinbase, which would become the largest U.S.-based cryptocurrency exchange. Meanwhile, the Winklevoss twins, Tyler and Cameron, launched a cryptocurrency exchange named Gemini, which would go on to become a top exchange. The brothers used a chunk of their $65 million legal settlement from Mark Zuckerberg, whom they accused of stealing their idea for Facebook, to invest heavily in Bitcoin a few years earlier when it was only $120 per coin. That daring investment ultimately made them billionaires.

The year 2015 also saw the coming of a second Satoshi Nakamoto-type visionary. On July 30, 2015, Russian-Canadian prodigy Vitalik Buterin (Figure 4.3) launched Ethereum, an ambitious cryptocurrency project that sought to be a second-generation upgrade of Bitcoin. Ethereum enabled developers to program their own smart contracts, facilitating the exchange of money, property, shares or anything of value without a middleman. As with Bitcoin, many cryptocurrency projects have been built off of the Ethereum platform. Ethereum now ranks as the No. 2 cryptocurrency in terms of marketcap behind only Bitcoin.

Buterin is definitely someone to keep an eye on in the cryptoverse. At age 17, he co-founded *Bitcoin Magazine*, one of the first and most-respected cryptocurrency publications. At 21, he launched Ethereum. In 2018, *Vice News* dubbed him "the blockchain's movement's biggest celebrity."[19] Only 24-years-old, he's a rising star who probably has more good ideas to come. Some experts speculate that a "flippening" may occur in the next couple

Figure 4.3 Vitalik Buterin
Source: Crypto maniacs Sergej Kunz and Anton Bukov

years, and Ethereum could replace Bitcoin as the gold standard for crypto-currency. For now, Bitcoin continues to reign supreme.

2017: cryptocurrency's golden age

In fact, 2017 brought unprecedented growth for Bitcoin. The granddaddy of cryptocurrencies began 2017 worth about $1,000 per coin. A major Bitcoin milestone occurred in March 2017 when one Bitcoin hit $1,200 and over-took the price of an ounce of gold. Bitcoin's price continued to skyrocket for the next 10 months, as many new investors jumped in due to FOMO, an acronym that means fear of missing out. Riding Bitcoin's coattails, the entire cryptocurrency market flourished with more than 1,000 cryptocur-rencies being sold on exchanges – many attaining incredible profit margins.

By June 2017, one Bitcoin was worth nearly $3,000 and the total mar-ketcap for cryptocurrency hit $100 billion. Bitcoin's price continued to rise rapidly. In late November, it hit $10,000 for the very first time, a tenfold increase from the beginning of the year. On December 17, 2017, Bitcoin set a new record that's yet to be broken. It hit nearly $20,000 per coin. Meanwhile, the total marketcap for cryptocurrency peaked shortly after that at around $800 billion. If cryptocurrency can be said to have had a golden age in its young life, 2017 was definitely it. But the quick, parabolic gains worried many financial experts, including Warren Buffett who warned that cryptocurrency was "a bubble" that would end badly. He may have been right.

2018: recession yet optimism

Early in 2018, the market came tumbling down. A series of disconcerting events, including new government regulations in many Asian countries and a bankruptcy court ordering MtGox to liquidate its remaining 100,000 Bitcoins to repay creditors, caused Bitcoin's price – along with the cryptocurrency market – to enter a great recession. By Summer 2018, the price of Bitcoin had dipped below $6,000 and the total cryptocurrency market had shrunk to about $250 million, illustrating the fear, uncertainty and doubt (or "FUD") that continue to surround cryptocurrency.

"The bubble has been popped. Bull market in $BTC over for some time," tweeted renowned commodity trading expert Peter Brandt.[20] *New York Post* business columnist John Crudele declared Bitcoin would never recover. It's a "fake currency, which I like to call Bitcon," he said. It's a "Ponzi scheme. Confidence game. Fraud. . . . Bitcoin is headed for a value of zilch. It's only a matter of when."[21] Many agree with these dire forecasts. "Cryptocurrency is ultimately an experiment that for all intents and purposes failed," cybersecurity expert Ross Rustici said. "It never achieved acceptance as a fiat currency that has intrinsic value on its own, and the marketplace is too unpredictable and prone to disruptions."[22] Nouriel Roubini, economics professor of New York University's Stern School of Business, called cryptocurrency the "biggest bubble in human history," comparing it to the 17th-century tulip crisis.[23]

Admittedly, there are many reasons to be bearish about cryptocurrency's future. More regulation is likely globally and locally. Government officials in the United States and Europe have stated on several recent occasions that stricter regulations are needed. Some governments such as Pakistan have already outlawed their citizens owning Bitcoin. In the long term, more government oversight might help stabilize cryptocurrency's volatile market and attract risk-averse institutional investors with deep pockets. But, initially, it usually causes FUD that sends cryptocurrency prices plunging.

To make matters worse, corporate America – perhaps trying to protect customers from scams or perhaps threatened by the disruption cryptocurrency could bring to their business models – has also hindered adoption. Some American banks won't allow their customers to transfer funds to cryptocurrency exchanges. Google and Facebook, the world's largest digital advertising platforms, banned cryptocurrency ads for a period before later allowing them again.

Despite these obstacles and ominous predictions, a number of recent developments have many investors expecting a turnaround. A 2018 study found that while only 9% owned cryptocurrency at the moment, the number investing was expected to almost triple in the near future.[24] Goldman Sachs announced plans to open a crypto trading desk. BlackRock and Facebook expressed interest in venturing into cryptocurrency as well. The Marshall Islands enacted a law that replaces the U.S. dollar with its own cryptocurrency as the country's official currency. Bitcoin exploded in popularity in developing nations as political turmoil sent several devastated nations' economies and sent their citizens scrambling for better investment alternatives. Bitcoin transactions hit record highs in Venezuela and Turkey during 2018. Meanwhile, in Iran, Bitcoin's price spiked to a world record $24,000 on local exchanges in September. While the news in America wasn't as positive, it's important to keep in mind that 2018 was a rough year for U.S. tech stocks as well. By December, Facebook, Apple, Amazon, Netflix and Google lost nearly $1 trillion in value from their year-long highs – more than the entire cryptocurrency market combined.

Just as the tech stocks will eventually rebound, cryptocurrency enthusiasts expect the same for their investments. They are quick to remind everyone of Bitcoin's previous crashes and multiple comebacks. "There have always been booms and busts in various financial markets, especially as new assets are invented," notes Andrei Kirilenko, director of the Centre for Global Finance and Technology at Imperial College Business School in London.[25]

Whether Bitcoin someday reaches $100,000 or goes to zero like many tech stocks did following the irrational exuberance of the dot-com boom is anyone's guess. Still, considering we're less than a decade on from cryptocurrency's implementation, it seems likely that we're just seeing the start of adoption for this bold idea. If there's one thing Bitcoin's history (Figure 4.4) has consistently demonstrated, it's that it is resilient (see Table 4.1).

"A lot of people are focused on the price but the important thing to remember is the fundamentals haven't changed," said Anthony Pompliano, founder of Morgan Creek Capital Management.

> If you look at the technicals for the historical analysis these bear markets continue to get deeper. We've had two of them previously and this one looks like it could go down to $3,000 [per Bitcoin] . . . but I don't think people should be surprised if that happens. It doesn't change the historical or long-term outlook. . . . This is still a nascent technology, it's only 10-years-old. But it's been the best performing asset over the past 10 years. It's beaten stocks, bonds, commodities and currencies. . . . So, we have a positive sentiment.[26]

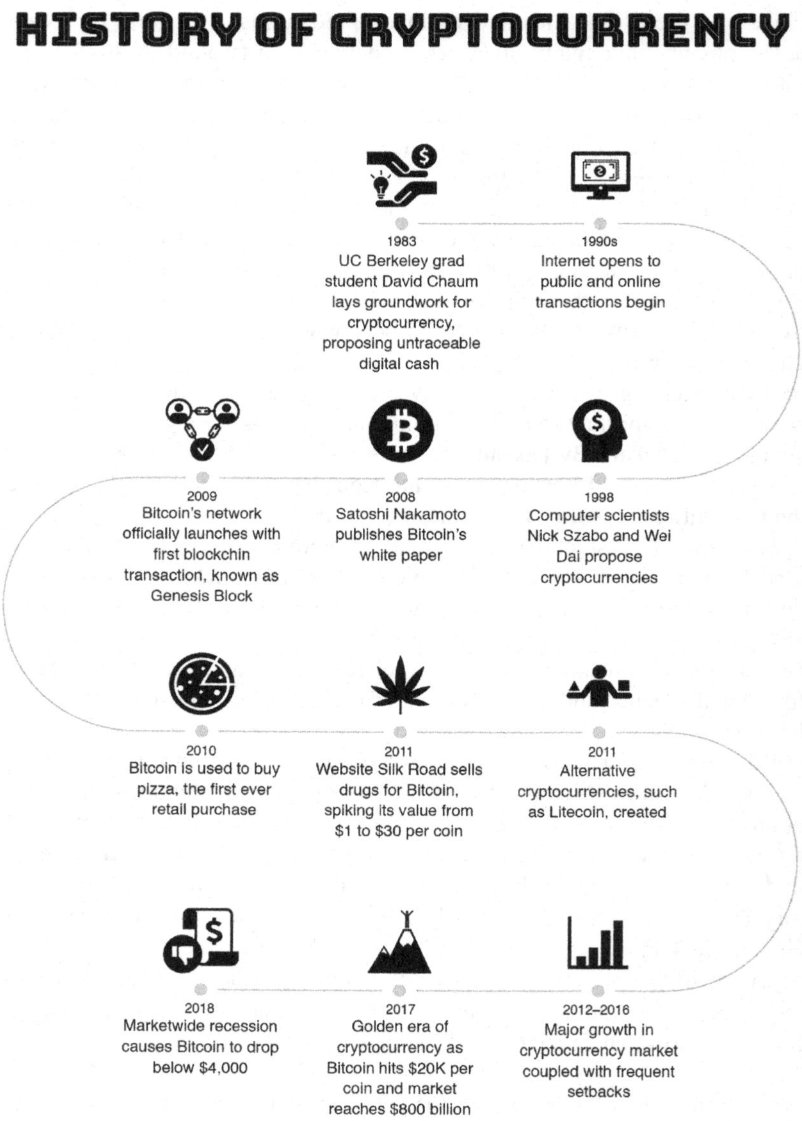

HISTORY OF CRYPTOCURRENCY

1983
UC Berkeley grad student David Chaum lays groundwork for cryptocurrency, proposing untraceable digital cash

1990s
Internet opens to public and online transactions begin

2009
Bitcoin's network officially launches with first blockchin transaction, known as Genesis Block

2008
Satoshi Nakamoto publishes Bitcoin's white paper

1998
Computer scientists Nick Szabo and Wei Dai propose cryptocurrencies

2010
Bitcoin is used to buy pizza, the first ever retail purchase

2011
Website Silk Road sells drugs for Bitcoin, spiking its value from $1 to $30 per coin

2011
Alternative cryptocurrencies, such as Litecoin, created

2018
Marketwide recession causes Bitcoin to drop below $4,000

2017
Golden era of cryptocurrency as Bitcoin hits $20K per coin and market reaches $800 billion

2012–2016
Major growth in cryptocurrency market coupled with frequent setbacks

Figure 4.4 History of cryptocurrency

Table 4.1 Bitcoin: major corrections (September 2010–June 2018)

Correction Period	# Days	Bitcoin High	Bitcoin Low	% Decline	% Return to New High	New High Date	# Days to New High
12/17/17 to 6/22/2018	187	19,783	5,938	–70%	233%	?	?
11/8/17 to 11/12/17	4	7,879	5,507	–30%	43%	11/16/2017	8
9/2/2017 to 9/15/17	13	5,014	2,951	–41%	70%	10/12/2017	40
6/11/2017 to 7/16/2017	35	3,025	1,837	–39%	65%	8/5/2017	55
3/10/2017 to 3/24/2017	14	1,326	892	–33%	49%	4/27/2017	48
11/30/2013 to 1/14/2015	410	1,166	170	–85%	585%	2/23/2017	1181
4/10/2013 to 7/7/2013	88	266	63	–76%	323%	11/7/2013	211
6/8/2011 to 11/17/2011	162	32	1.99	–94%	1,504%	2/28/2013	631
5/13/2011 to 5/21/2011	8	8.45	5.58	–34%	51%	5/25/2011	12
2/10/2011 to 4/4/2011	53	1.10	0.56	–49%	96%	4/17/2011	66
11/6/2010 to 11/10/2010	4	0.50	0.14	–72%	257%	1/31/2011	86
9/14/2010 to 10/8/2010	24	0.17	0.01	–94%	1,600%	10/24/2010	40

Source: Charlie Bilello/Pension Partners

Data Source: CoinDesk

Notes

1 Marissa Fessenden, "What Was the First Thing Sold on the Internet?" *Smithsonian.com* (Nov. 30, 2015), available at www.smithsonianmag.com/smart-news/what-was-first-thing-sold-internet-180957414/.

2 Aaron van Wirdum, "The Genesis Files: How David Chaum's eCash Spawned a Cypherpunk Dream," *Bitcoin Magazine* (Apr. 24, 2018), available at https://bitcoinmagazine.com/articles/genesis-files-how-david-chaums-ecash-spawned-cypherpunk-dream/.

3 See supra note 2 (van Wirdum).

4 Charles Dearing, "Nobel Laureate Milton Friedman Predicted Bitcoin Era 17 Years Ago," *Cointelegraph* (July 7, 2017), available at https://cointelegraph.com/news/nobel-laureate-milton-friedman-predicted-bitcoin-era-17-years-ago.

5 Satoshi Nakamoto, "Bitcoin: A Peer-to-Peer Electronic Cash System," *Bitcoin Project* (Oct. 31, 2008), available at https://bitcoin.org/bitcoin.pdf.

6 Hassnain Javed, "21st-Century Unicorn: Or the Future?" *The Nation* (Jan. 18, 2018), available at https://nation.com.pk/18-Jan-2018/21st-century-unicorn-or-the-future.

7 John Bohannon, "The Bitcoin Busts," *Science* (Mar. 11, 2016), available at http://science.sciencemag.org/content/351/6278/1144.

8 Kari Stray, "Who Created Bitcoin: Long Story Short," *Cointelegraph* (July 17, 2017), available at https://cointelegraph.com/news/who-created-bitcoin-long-story-short.

9 Lionel Shriver, "Why Cryptocurrency Is the Answer," *The Spectator* (Jan. 6, 2018), available at www.spectator.co.uk/2018/01/why-cryptocurrencies-are-the-answer/.

10 Rainey Reitman, "Bitcoin: A Step toward Censorship-Resistant Digital Currency," *Electronic Frontier Foundation* (Jan. 20, 2011), available at www.eff.org/deeplinks/2011/01/bitcoin-step-toward-censorship-resistant.

11 Jerry Brito, "Online Cash Bitcoin Could Challenge Governments, Banks," *Time* (Apr. 16, 2011), available at http://techland.time.com/2011/04/16/online-cash-bitcoin-could-challenge-governments/2/.

12 Robin O'Connell, "Why Does Bitcoin Have Value," *The Daily Hodl* (Oct. 30, 2018), available at https://dailyhodl.com/2018/10/30/why-does-bitcoin-have-value/.

13 Sherwin Dowlat, "ICO Quality: Development & Trading," *Satis Group* (Mar. 21, 2018), available at https://medium.com/satis-group/ico-quality-development-trading-e4fef28df04f.

14 Robert McMillan, "California Says the Bitcoin Foundation Is a Money-Transferrer," *Wired* (June 24, 2013), available at www.wired.com/2013/06/california_dfi/.

15 Matthew J. Belvedere, "Everyone Online! Google's Schmidt on Benefits and Risks," *CNBC* (Apr. 23, 2013), available at www.cnbc.com/id/100663780.

16 Richard Branson, "How Digital Currency Could Transform the World," *Virgin* (Nov. 13, 2014), available at www.virgin.com/richard-branson/how-digital-currency-could-transform-the-world.

17 Tim Worstall, "It's Not That Bitcoin Can Be Regulated as Money: It's That Now Bitcoin Will Be Regulated as Money," *Forbes* (Aug. 8, 2013), available at www.forbes.com/sites/timworstall/2013/08/08/its-not-that-bitcoin-can-be-regulated-as-money-its-that-now-bitcoin-will-be-regulated-as-money/#445ec24f163c.

18 Zachary M. Seward, "Ben Bernanke's Letter to Congress: Bitcoin and Other Virtual Currencies 'May Hold Long-Term Promise'," *Quartz* (Nov. 18, 2013), available at https://qz.com/148399/ben-bernanke-bitcoin-may-hold-long-term-promise/.

19 N.A., "We Met the Founder of Ethereum," *Vice News* (Apr. 22, 2018), available at www.facebook.com/vicenews/videos/we-met-the-founder-of-ethereum-vice-on-hbo/1019175654909051/.

20 Peter Brandt, tweet via @PeterLBrandt account, *Twitter* (Dec. 21, 2017), available at https://twitter.com/PeterLBrandt/status/944027711881715714.

21 John Crudele, "Why Bitcoin May Soon Be Worth Nothing," *New York Post* (July 4, 2018), available at https://nypost.com/2018/07/04/why-bitcoin-may-be-soon-worth-nothing/.

22 Sean Keach, "Bitcoin Blasted as a 'Failed Experiment' after Huge 70% Price Crash," *The Sun* (July 5, 2018), available at www.thesun.co.uk/tech/6686173/bitcoin-price-crash-scam-cryptocurrency-dead-value-worth-high/.

23 David Cowan, "Cryptocurrency Regulation becomes a Top Priority," *Raconteur* (June 25, 2018), available at www.raconteur.net/finance/cryptocurrency-regulation-top-priority.

24 Ana Alexandre, "ING Bank Survey Reveals Interest in Crypto Will Double in Near Future," *Cointelegraph* (June 27, 2018), available at https://cointelegraph.com/news/ing-bank-survey-reveals-interest-in-crypto-will-double-in-near-future.

25 See supra note 23 (Cowan).

26 Anthony Pompliano, interview, *CNN* (Nov. 23, 2018), available at https://twitter.com/APompliano/status/1066058486851739648.

5 Investing

Cryptocurrencies are arguably the hottest investment product currently available. But with approximately 2,000 types for sale, a din of information online and a market that never sleeps, how does a new investor navigate the rapidly evolving world of cryptocurrency?

This chapter covers how to invest in cryptocurrency: how to decide which coins to invest in; how to acquire coins; how to send, spend and receive coins; how to sell coins; and how to convert them back to cash. You'll also learn how to protect your investment from thieves, scammers and hackers. There's also a list of the most trustworthy exchanges worldwide, along with a detailed analysis of Bitcoin, Ethereum and ten of the most popular and promising alternative coins.

But before we cover why and how to invest, let's first consider why perhaps you shouldn't invest.

Crypto isn't for everyone

Just because you're reading this book on cryptocurrency doesn't mean you have to invest in it. There's value in simply understanding what the Bitcoin and blockchain craze is all about. And, after weighing the benefits against the risks, you might decide cryptocurrency isn't for you – if so, no worries!

Cryptocurrency is intimidating, complicated, risky and highly volatile.

Cryptoland can be intimidating due to the complexities in understanding the cutting-edge technology. The use of technical computing terms can confuse and deter outsiders. It requires time and energy to wrap your head around.

Even if you understand it, there's no guarantee of success when it comes to investing. It takes a special investor who can deal with the extreme price fluctuations, prevalent scams, uncertain legal future and other risks associated with cryptocurrency. It also takes luck. Yes, there's potential to make a lot of money quickly. But there's also a good chance you could just as quickly lose everything you invest.

Cryptocurrency is highly volatile. Take a look at the price history of Bitcoin in Table 5.1, and you'll see that it's frequently in flux; there are significant rises and falls in short periods of time. As Bitcoin goes, so goes the cryptocurrency market as a whole. This market is much more volatile and unpredictable than the stock market. Unlike the 9-to-5 New York Stock Exchange, cryptocurrency is traded around the world 24/7. So you may go to bed at night feeling pretty happy about your portfolio only to wake up the next day and see you've dropped 25% overnight. Bad news may break in Asia about a new government regulation, exchange hack or some other setback that hurts a particular coin or even causes a market-wide drop. Cryptocurrency does not take bad news well.

The year 2018 provides a cautionary tale. Many new investors entered the market in early January 2018, after Bitcoin hit an all-time high of nearly $20,000 in late December 2017. Unfortunately, following a constant parade of bad news (government regulation, exchange hacks, scams, disquieting rumors, etc.), Bitcoin steadily declined from the beginning of 2018 and

Table 5.1 Table of Bitcoin's price changes over time

Date	Price
Dec. 5, 2018	$3,928
July 25, 2018	$8,352
June 29, 2018	$5,917
May 5, 2018	$9,822
Feb. 6, 2018	$6,172
Dec. 12, 2017	$19,783
Sept. 15, 2017	$3,019
Aug. 31, 2017	$4,814
Jan. 1, 2017	$996
Jan. 2, 2016	$432
Jan. 17, 2015	$195
June 3, 2014	$669
April 10, 2014	$362
Nov. 30, 2013	$1,127

Source: CoinMarketCap.com

dropped all the way down to below $6,000 by July 2018. That means, new investors lost a lot of money in a short period of time. So, be forewarned that you're taking a risk by investing in cryptocurrency. And the more you invest, the bigger the risk. That's why cryptocurrency is often compared to gambling.

If you're generally cautious with your money and prefer stable, long-term investments that will steadily increase, there are much better investment avenues than cryptocurrency. Even Vitalik Buterin, the founder of Ethereum, the No. 2 ranked cryptocurrency in the world, conceded in a tweet: "Reminder: cryptocurrencies are still a new and hyper-volatile asset class, and could drop to near-zero at any time. Don't put in more money than you can afford to lose. If you're trying to figure out where to store your life savings, traditional assets are still your safest bet."[1]

And here's the kicker: even when the cryptocurrency market is going well, you may lose your investment other ways. Unlike banks, credit cards or stock exchanges, there are no fail safes in cryptocurrency to protect your funds. It's entirely up to you to take the necessary steps to ensure the security of your cryptocurrency investments. If you forget your private key, transfer funds to the wrong address or get hacked, no one will be able to help you, and you may not be able to recover your losses.

Sound stressful? It certainly can be. But try not to take cryptocurrency too seriously. If you do not learn to be easy going about risks and losses, you will drive yourself crazy. At the same time, do not treat it as a casino or lottery. You need to have a sound strategy and strong sense of purpose to succeed in the cryptocurrency market. Always be skeptical and cautious.

Why invest?

The fact that most people would be intimidated by what I just told you is the very reason why you should consider getting into cryptocurrency. Jumping on the bandwagon earlier than most will give you an edge, both in terms of experience and potential gains. Admittedly, it can be a steep learning curve. But it will all be worth it if cryptocurrency ultimately succeeds. The hope is that once there's more mainstream coverage of cryptocurrencies and their potential, the large institutions and mass population will start pouring in. In fact, it's already starting to happen. So, if you learn the ropes of cryptocurrency investing now, you might reap sweet rewards in the near future.

Although investors who entered the market in 2018 got "rekt," those who invested a year earlier experienced astounding gains. For example, in 2017, Bitcoin increased from about $900 to $20,000 per coin. Ethereum, meanwhile, grew from approximately $10 to $1,400 per coin. And NEO went from 36 cents to $160! Even after the major market downturn in

2018, those early investments would have still paid off handsomely. As of December 2018, Bitcoin was about $4,000 per coin (a $3,100 increase from early 2017); Ethereum was about $120 per coin (a $110 increase per coin since early 2017); and NEO was around $8 per coin (a $7.50 increase). These kinds of returns are impossible to acquire within the realm of traditional investments. Hopefully, 2018 was just a temporary setback – worse setbacks have happened on multiple occasions before in cryptocurrency's young history – and the market will experience new all-time highs in 2019 or 2020. To have a chance to reap these great rewards, you have to jump in and take the plunge.

This market is still in its infancy, and if you invest now, you can enjoy bragging rights if it takes off. Imagine having the opportunity to be part of the Internet revolution in the 1990s. It was a once-in-a-generation opportunity to acquire a vast amount of wealth and, more importantly, bragging rights – the legacy of being an early backer of a revolutionary technology. How many people can claim they took part in the development of such an innovation? Very few. Similar bragging rights are arguably at your fingertips now with cryptocurrency. The crypto world is blossoming to be a real game-changer in the evolution of money and tech. As we speak, applications are being developed to disrupt the current status quo for the better.

Finally, there are ideological reasons to invest. If you're not a big fan of the government, big banks or monopolistic corporations, then cryptocurrency may be a good fit for you. Let's face it, humans are used to having a central authority – in the form of a boss, an organization or a government – that sets rules for how things should operate. But what if the tables were turned and the masses had a real say in how things should be done? That would be a truly democratic system. Well, cryptocurrencies offer that by eliminating traditional powers and empowering the masses through decentralization. With widespread adoption of cryptocurrencies, people will no longer have to depend on financial institutions for transferring their money at an exorbitant fee. There are cryptocurrencies that allow users to transfer money to anyone at any place at any time at no cost. Not only that but also being able to privately and securely store your cryptocurrency gives you full control of your money. It's like managing your own bank; you make your own rules.

Consequently, as discussed in earlier chapters, many smart and successful people are optimistic about the future of cryptocurrency.

How much to invest?

OK, ready to take a leap of faith and invest? Follow the golden rule of investing: only invest what you can afford to lose. There's a natural tendency to want to overreach, thinking high risk can lead to high reward. But be smart and cautious. Don't run up credit card debt, take a 401K loan or remortgage your house to invest in cryptocurrency. The market is highly volatile, and your investment could go to zero. In addition, don't put all your disposable income into cryptocurrency. You should diversify your investments and invest in stocks, bonds, retirement plans, etc. Many investment experts recommend putting only a small fraction of your investment funds into the crypto market.

> **Only invest what you can afford to lose!**

Even if you have lots of money to gamble with, initially, you should just invest a little bit until you learn how to navigate the exchanges and get a feel for the market. Although Bitcoin is quite expensive, with a single coin costing several thousand dollars, you don't need to be rich to invest in cryptocurrency. You don't have to buy a whole Bitcoin; you can buy a very small fraction of a Bitcoin. There are also hundreds of other cryptocurrencies you can invest in, and some cost less than a penny per coin (although, like penny stocks, penny coins rarely make you rich).

Which cryptocurrencies to buy?

Begin by investing conservatively and only purchasing established, blue chip cryptocurrencies, such as Bitcoin and Ethereum. These are the two largest cryptocurrency projects and have a real case use. Moreover, you usually need to buy one or the other before you can purchase other coins. Like Forex, a popular online exchange for trading traditional currencies such as dollars and euros, cryptocurrencies are traded in pairs. When you purchase a cryptocurrency other than Bitcoin or Ethereum, its value is usually in relation to one of these two major coins.

After you gain some experience managing a portfolio with the big two cryptocurrencies and have had time to conduct research and study the market, you might foray into other coins such as Litecoin, Cardano, Stellar or one of the other hundreds of alternative coins. Or you might not. Many successful investors play it safe and stick with Bitcoin and Ethereum (which are often referred to by their abbreviations, BTC and ETH). It's easier to make quick gains with alternative coins (or "altcoins"), but it's also a lot easier to lose your shirt. Disciplined, cautious long-term investing in blue chip coins has proven to be the safest way to grow your portfolio, and it benefits the entire cryptocurrency market. Throwing money at unproven, risky altcoins is what leads to speculation that the cryptocurrency market is a bubble about to burst.

Check out this book's companion website, CryptocurrencyText book.com, which has short videos that walk you through step-by-step how to buy cryptocurrency.

How to buy

Numerous ways exist to invest in and start buying cryptocurrency.

First, you'll need an online bank account that allows you to wire money to cryptocurrency exchanges. Some exchanges, such as Coinbase, also allow you to buy cryptocurrency using a credit card, although I wouldn't recommend taking on credit card debt to buy cryptocurrency. Be aware that your bank may charge a fee for wiring money. A few banks and credit cards also prohibit their customers from sending funds to cryptocurrency exchanges.

Second, you'll need to have government IDs ready (such as a driver's license and perhaps a passport) to verify your identity on most legitimate exchanges. Many U.S. and European exchanges abide by KYC regulations, which exist to prevent cryptocurrency from being used by criminals for money laundering activities.

Third, choose your exchange. There are dozens of cryptocurrency exchanges and new ones opening each week. Not all of them are reliable and trustworthy. Avoid shady exchanges (more on this later). Only use well-known exchanges that provide good security and easy liquidity. I personally prefer using an American online cryptocurrency exchange, such as Coinbase. It is fairly easy-to-use, secure, has a good reputation and is among the few exchanges regulated by government agencies in the United States. Coinbase allows customers from the U.S., Canada, United Kingdom, Europe, Singapore and Australia buy cryptocurrency with a credit card or bank account. Foreign exchanges with strong reputations include Bitpanda (Europe), Bitfinex (Hong Kong), Huobi (Singapore), UPbit (South Korea) and Coinmama (Europe).

You will then register your personal information (name, address, government ID number, etc.); verify your identity by uploading cell phone pictures of your government IDs; deposit your local currency, such as dollars or euros; and, finally, be able to purchase Bitcoin or Ethereum at the current rate of exchange. If you decide to sell any of your cryptocurrency, it is quite simple on these exchanges, and you can send your money back to your bank account in a matter of days (it would be quicker, but banks are sometimes slow processing). Be aware that any time you make a transaction on an exchange (whether it's to buy, sell or trade cryptocurrency), there will likely be transaction or commission fees. These fees vary by exchange but are usually around 1%.

After you've become more experienced and knowledgeable in the crypto space, and you're ready to invest in altcoins, use a well-known altcoin exchange such as the U.S.-based Bittrex or Malta-based Binance, the world's most popular exchange. Both offer a wide selection of altcoins, have good reputations, strong security and I've personally used them countless times without any problems. But note, these exchanges do not accept direct fiat deposits and instead require Bitcoin or Ethereum deposits to purchase altcoins. While fiat-accepting exchanges such as Coinbase sell altcoins, their selection is much more limited. I wouldn't mess with decentralized exchanges, such as IDEX or EtherDelta, until you're a very seasoned trader. While such exchanges offer certain advantages (e.g., they're arguably safer from hackers, more anonymous and offer the chance to buy small market-cap hidden gems before they hit big exchanges), they tend to be clunky and quite complicated to use if you're a new investor – and quite easy to botch transactions on.

Investing in altcoins

As you've probably surmised by now, the term "altcoins" refers to coins that are an alternative to Bitcoin or Ethereum (although some Bitcoin enthusiasts would probably insist that anything other than Bitcoin is an altcoin). Sometimes altcoins are just called "coins." Altcoins represent a good way to achieve significant profits, but they're also more complicated to trade. So, before we discuss investing strategies, let's first cover some background information.

Many altcoins are a variant (or "fork") of Bitcoin, built using its open-sourced, original protocol with changes to its underlying code, thus producing an entirely new coin with different features. For example, Litecoin is an altcoin based on Bitcoin's code that conducts transactions more quickly. Bitcoin Private is an altcoin that offers more anonymity in transactions. There are also altcoins that aren't derived from Bitcoin's open-source code. Rather, such altcoins have created from scratch their own code and blockchain that supports their native currency. Examples of these altcoins include Ethereum, Ripple and NEO. These three coins are among the biggest competitors to Bitcoin – although Bitcoin is by far the big dog (for now – there could come a day when "the Flippening" occurs and a competitor overtakes Bitcoin as the top coin).

Besides Bitcoin and altcoins, there is also a third type of cryptocurrency known as tokens. Tokens differ from other cryptocurrencies in their structure. Instead of having their own separate blockchain, tokens operate on top of an existing blockchain that facilitates the creation of decentralized applications (DApps). For example, Basic Attention Token (BAT) is an Ethereum token that aims to improve digital advertising. Narrative (NRV) is a NEO token that aims to incentivize social media influencers.

As of 2018, there were more than 2,000 cryptocurrencies – and that number will likely only increase. While a small minority of them will skyrocket in value or "moon," most are "shitcoins," meaning they will falter and eventually go to zero. (Please excuse the crudeness, but the crypto space is not known for its etiquette and foul language is part of the common vernacular.) In fact, many of these coins are considered "dead coins" or "abandonware," which means they no longer have developers who are actively working to build and improve them. (Once in a great while, a dead coin might be revived into something with potential, but it's rare and an extremely risky investment.) Prominent blockchain experts have warned that 90% of all cryptocurrencies will fail, and we should therefore invest with great caution.

Given this, how does an investor decide which altcoins are worth investing in? By conducting a fundamental analysis (FA). This involves researching to assess a coin's viability and potential.

Conducting a fundamental analysis

First, look at whether the coin has much room to grow. When researching altcoins and tokens, pay close attention to their marketcap and coin supply. The higher those are, the less room there is for growth.

A FA involves researching a coin's white paper, purpose, team, partnerships, roadmap and more to assess its viability and potential.

The **marketcap** is calculated by multiplying the total number of coins by its current price. So, a cryptocurrency that is valued at $10 per coin and has a 100-million-coin supply will have a total marketcap of $1 billion.

Coin supply is important, too. This is the total number of units of a particular cryptocurrency. For example, there are 21 million Bitcoins and 100 million Ethereum. There are more than a billion coins each of Ripple, Stellar, Tron and Cardano. Consequently, a single Ripple (which also goes by the symbol XRP), Stellar (XLM), Tron (TRX) or Cardano (ADA) will never be worth $1,000 or anywhere near as much as a single Bitcoin. Even if these altcoins with enormous coin supplies achieved Bitcoin's marketcap (which they probably won't), a single one of those altcoins would only be worth perhaps $5 to $10 each.

That said, it's easier for a new coin with a small marketcap (say $10 million) to triple or even 100× in price than it is for an established coin with a huge marketcap (say $1 billion plus) to do so. The smaller a coin's marketcap, the more upside it has. So, there is profit to be made off of cheaper coins with huge coin supplies – but you'll have to buy a lot of them to realize huge gains.

A mistake many new investors make is investing in a coin simply because the price per coin is cheap(er). For example, imagine we're deciding between two coins: Coin X and Coin Y. Coin X has a supply of 1,000 coins worth $1 each while Coin Y has a supply of ten coins worth $100 each. The value of both cryptocurrencies is exactly the same, as they both have the same marketcap. However, many people automatically assume that investing in Coin X is a better choice. Not necessarily. Here's why: the more coins there are, the less special they are. Owning one rare painting from a good artist is often better than owning 100 paintings from mediocre artists.

Also, keep in mind that a cryptocurrency's coin supply can change, so that may impact its price down the road. "Circulating supply" is the number of coins that are circulating in the market. "Total supply" is the total amount of coins in existence right now (minus any coins that have been verifiably burned. Sometimes a cryptocurrency project will reduce its coin supply to make it rarer and thus hopefully raise its value. This is known as a burn). "Max supply" is the maximum number of coins that will ever exist in the lifetime of the cryptocurrency.

A coin's supply can be inflationary, which means its total number of coins will increase over time; it can be deflationary, which means it will decrease its supply over time; or it can be stagnant, which means its supply always remains constant. Bitcoin is an example of an inflationary coin (until its 21 million max supply is reached; there are currently about 17 million in circulation now), Quantum (QUA) is an example of a deflationary coin and NEO is an example of a coin that is neither.

Another important consideration is **volume**. This is how much money is being spent on trades involving the coin in the past 24 hours. This is important because a coin with low volume may be difficult to sell at its listed price. You may be able to get a coin at an attractive price, but later be unable to sell all the coins you have purchased. Legitimate coins tend to consistently have at least a half-million-dollar volume per day. That said, when a coin is newly launched, it may only be listed on one small exchange and thus have low volume (under $100,000). The newer the coin, the more tolerable low volume is. Be wary of older coins with low volume, as they could be difficult to unload and heading toward shit coin territory.

To reiterate: marketcap, coin supply and volume are a few of the most important factors to look at when conducting a FA. But they are not the only factors you should consider when trying to find a good investment in the cryptocurrency market. Beyond those three things, also look at these factors:

1   **White paper**: This is a detailed written proposal by the coin's employees that explains the purpose and mechanics of the coin. The white paper is the main source of evaluating a coin's fundamentals. You should always read it before investing, although it's not always easy reading given the use of specialized jargon and technical concepts. If a coin doesn't have a white paper or if it's been plagiarized (yes, this happens more often than you might think), I'd avoid investing, as lack of a good, original white paper suggests the coin's founders are either clueless or scammers.

2   **Purpose**: The coin must have a useful functional benefit. Look for coins that offer a product that solves an important need or issue related to blockchain – many projects are just duplicates of existing projects. This isn't to say that some pointless projects won't pump (increase in value), but they will invariably dump (get sold off) as soon as speculators lose interest. This is what causes the market's current volatility and talks of a cryptocurrency bubble. As with the dot-com boom and bust, the crypto space features many companies that add no value.

To avoid a company that's likely to fail, here are some questions to ask when judging a coin's utility potential: Is there a real-world problem that the company is trying to solve? Will their proposed solution significantly improve the way things are done? Will the coin attached to this project provide functionality which only a cryptocurrency can deliver? What is the tangible benefit of using a cryptocurrency for this solution as opposed to a non-blockchain technology? Assuming that 90% of projects will fail, why do you believe this cryptocurrency will still exist in five years' time?

Let's consider two real examples: Dogecoin (DOGE) was created as a "parody" coin in 2013. As such, the coin serves no particular purpose, brings no technological advancements and solves no real-world problem (no offense to DOGE owners!). It has not been updated in over two years, yet it still has a marketcap of nearly $300 million (and even reached $1 billion during early 2018). DOGE's value is entirely derived from supply and demand and people's perception of its price. On the other hand, Ethereum (ETH) has obvious value. In addition to its price being derived from speculators' perception, ETH is also used to pay for implementing and executing smart contracts on the

Ethereum network. Therefore, ETH is backed by the value that these smart contracts provide.

I am not arguing that you should never invest in coins like DOGE, as they can bring a significant return on investment (ROI) in the short-term. But they are definitely riskier investments and more prone to eventually disappear than coins with real utility like ETH. So, at the very least, you should avoid coins like DOGE until you've been trading cryptocurrency for a while.

3   **Team**: Look for coins that have an accomplished staff behind them. Does the team have any prior experience in the industry the project is tackling? Sound projects will list team members on their website along with their credentials. If the team is very small (sometimes just one person is behind an entire project) or if members names aren't listed, or if they have scant credentials, be wary. There are exceptions. For instance, sometimes privacy coins will hide who's behind the project for obvious reasons (it's a privacy coin!). But there's no reason for, say, a token related to eSports to be secretive about its team. Speaking of the team, also look at what percentage of the cryptocurrency they hold. If this is a significant percentage (let's say over 25%–30%), question why. This could indicate that the founders created the project mainly to get rich quickly rather than because they truly believe in their idea. Do the founders have a valid reason for holding such a big amount of coins? If so, what are they planning to do with it?

4   **Investors and partnerships**: Something that can be helpful in gauging a project's likelihood of mass adoption is to examine its current investors and partnerships. Having the backing of well-established entities gives the project further legitimacy. A few examples of altcoins with eye-catching investors and partnerships are IOTA, which received investment from Robert Bosch Venture Capital and has a partnership with Volkswagen; Stellar (XLM), which has a partnership with IBM; and EchoLink (EKO), which has partnerships with Microsoft and LinkedIn.

5   **Roadmap**: Having an idea that can change the lives of eight billion people doesn't matter if it's never finished, or if it's finished and never used. Adoption strategy is the bridge between dreams and reality. It's the connector between ideas and results. So, take a look at the company's plan, which is commonly referred to as the "roadmap" in the crypto space. Does its roadmap outline a sound strategy toward gaining users? Is the company currently on track with its roadmap? Do they have a good track record of meeting their deadlines? Based on their experience, does the team demonstrate the ability to complete their roadmap?

6   **Public relations (PR) and marketing**: Too many cryptocurrency projects overlook the importance of public relations and marketing. Succeeding in this space is not all about tech. So much of a coin's adoption and value is driven by publicity. Consequently, some great projects struggle to gain traction because they lack PR. There's no point in creating a great product if nobody knows about it. So, check to make sure that a coin has a PR person who is active with social media outreach.

At the same time, don't be mindlessly seduced by PR – sometimes a slick marketing operation is employed to compensate for the fact that the underlying project is weak. Admittedly, some projects have taken off, despite being vaporware (i.e. they don't have a working product), because they're able to generate lots of buzz on social media. But eventually, these projects are exposed for the frauds they are and go to zero. Verge (XVG), for example, does a great job with promoting itself online. The hype often leads to the coin's price being "pumped." But the coin's underlying technology has encountered numerous problems, which has led to investors "dumping" the coin over and over again. At this point, most investors only buy the coin in hopes of making a quick buck; few experts believe in XVG's intrinsic value. XVG has seen its price dramatically increase and decrease in short periods several times, leading to it being labeled a "pump-and-dump" (P&D) coin.[2]

In closing, here's a final caveat: FA isn't a perfect science and involves some speculation (e.g., will this project be mass adopted?). But if you don't do your due diligence before investing, you're basically just guessing which coins to buy. Investment without FA is no better than gambling. I cannot emphasize enough how important it is to know what you are investing in. Knowledge is power.

Research

So, where can you find the info necessary to conduct a thorough FA? Here are some good resources:

1   **CoinMarketCap.com**: Also known simply as CMC, this free website provides an ever-growing list of cryptocurrencies that have been listed on exchanges along with info about each coin, including a link to its official website and market information, such as price, coin supply, marketcap and exchanges to buy it on. It also ranks all the coins by marketcap. Note that a coin's price on CMC is based on its average price across exchanges. In some cases, the price of a particular coin may vary by 10% or more depending on the exchange. Another good site for basic background info on a coin is MarketBeat.com/cryptocurrencies.

2   **The coin's website**: Legitimate projects have websites with a wealth of information. Be sure to study the coin maker's white paper, roadmap and team. If any of this information is missing, don't invest. It's no different than trusting your money with a random stranger. If there's an official blog or "news" section, you should also follow the updates given by the team.

3   **Competitors' websites**: Identify similar projects and compare their white papers, teams and roadmaps. Which project is most likely to succeed? For example, SALT and ETHLend are competitors. Both projects allow holders of cryptocurrency assets to leverage their holdings as collateral for cash loans. You don't want to bet on the figurative Betamax instead of VHS (or MySpace instead of Facebook), so do an FA and determine which project has the better chance to succeed.

4   **LinkedIn**: Look around the Internet at sites like LinkedIn to verify the team's credentials and check that members have achieved what they say they have. As with all fields, imposters abound in cryptoland.

5   **Google**: Search for anything that you can find about the company, especially news and interviews. Avoid rumors and pay attention instead to facts. If you find news, it will likely be from trade magazines and specialized sites, such as Cointelegraph, CoinDesk, the Block or CCN. By the time major mainstream media outlets such as the *New York Times* and CNBC report on a particular coin, it's often a "reverse indicator" (a sign that the coin's been overhyped and overbought). Note, when searching for info on a coin: people often refer to coins by their abbreviated symbols. Bitcoin's is BTC and $BTC. So, search for those terms as well.

6   **Ask their community**: Join the coin's Facebook Group, Telegram Chat or Discord Group and ask questions to fill in any knowledge gaps. If you're confused by the technical jargon, try asking your question along with the term "ELI5," which stands for "explain like I'm 5." But take community feedback with a grain of salt because members of these communities have a vested interest in convincing you to invest: if you buy, it helps raise the coin's demand and price.

Social media

Social media can also be useful for gathering intel. Twitter, online discussion forums such as Reddit, Bitcointalk and Steemit, along with videos on YouTube can all help you understand coins better, as well as the sentiments surrounding them. A coin's price can be largely driven by public opinion, and social media can provide a glimpse into what the crowd is thinking.

Be aware: blockchain companies often hire people to promote or "shill" their coin online. Simply having lots of social media buzz doesn't necessarily mean a project is good. In fact, some of the coins with the strongest social media campaigns have the worst products. On the other hand, sometimes a good project will initially fly low on the social media radar before it garners a lot of attention and buzz.

Also be aware: social media and online discussion forums are filled with so-called trolls. These are immature and hostile people who harass others for fun. It's important to have thick skin and not take any nasty comments too seriously or personally.

Take any information you learn from social media with a grain of salt. The cryptocurrency market is outrageously speculative and just about everyone has an opinion on how prices will move. You will see all sorts of conflicting information when trawling through Reddit, Twitter and other social media. Every day, there are many rumors (both good and bad news) posted online that more often than not turn out to be false. Trades made on the basis of this can lead to big losses and, unfortunately, this is something you will be exposed to as a new trader.

Even the so-called experts with 100,000-plus followers frequently give advice that's very hit-and-miss. I've followed several of the most popular crypto pundits on Twitter and discovered they constantly brag about their one big Hail Mary pick that mooned but neglect to mention – or delete – their numerous fumbles. Some of them even charge $1,000 per month to subscribe to their newsletter or participate in their private group. Rarely, if ever, is the price worth it.

Watch out for Twitter scammers offering to send you free Bitcoin or Ethereum.

Never invest in a coin because one person says to. On the other hand, never avoid investing in a coin just because someone said not to. Sometimes people intentionally lie and spread misinformation about a coin to help or hurt its price. Why do this? Because they're working for or heavily invested in the coin or a competing coin. Or simply because they're jerks who like to troll and spread disinformation. There are bad people out there who are looking to take advantage of naive newbies who invest blindly. So, crowd-source and do your own research.

As it goes with every hype, "everyone and his uncle" can become a guru during a bubble. Be very selective when following people and choosing sources to read. Social media has only a handful of people who are worth following – I'd estimate, maximum 2%. That said, there are some extremely knowledgeable people who frequently dispense good advice free of charge. Do your own research and identify who to trust.

A final word of caution about social media: it's full of scams. Scammers will often create imposter accounts and pose as well-known crypto people (such as Ethereum creator Vitalik Buterin or even the pope!). They'll say they're giving away free Ethereum if you just send them your private key or if you send them a fraction of an Ethereum (e.g., "I'll give you 10 ETH if you send me 0.1 ETH"). Don't fall for these scams. Almost no one gives away free cryptocurrency. If something seems too good to be true, it usually is.

To sum up social media: it's one way to gather intel on a coin you're considering buying, but it shouldn't be the be-all, end-all of deciding whether to invest.

Other investment strategies

Instead of diving deep into the principles of cryptocurrency and conducting an FA, some investors use other strategies to choose coins. The following are a few examples of other popular investment strategies – but I wouldn't recommend them, as they have flaws.

> **Follow the money**: Using this strategy, you buy a certain amount of different coins among the top-ten ranked cryptocurrencies on CMC. The idea is that at least some of the coins will skyrocket and that will offset losses from the failure of the other coins. But this strategy can have huge risks. Nothing can protect you from the possibility that what have been seemingly reliable coins thus far can considerably decrease in value next year. You should remember that right now, there are no fundamental grounds protecting a top-ten coin like Litecoin from falling. It's a close clone of Bitcoin that may ultimately prove unable to withstand the competition of other coins.
>
> **The "penny stocks" approach**: If you have some knowledge of the stock market, you should be familiar with the penny stocks approach. Basically, these are typically shares of a small, inconsequential company that nobody wants to own. However, these shares have one feature: they are so cheap that nothing prevents them from shooting up tenfold in value. Such a magical leap can occur because of good news, market manipulation or many other reasons.
>
> The cryptocurrency market is loaded with penny coins. In fact, many coins sell for a fraction of a penny. In order to take advantage

of this strategy in cryptocurrency, you would buy odd, obscure coins and then wait and see if anything develops. At some point during the year, the prices of your cheap coins may skyrocket. If you bought 25 different cryptocurrencies, a leap in the price of even one super-cheap coin will likely more than compensate for any losses in your entire investment portfolio. This strategy requires no skills or knowledge, only luck. Consequently, this is an ill-advised investment strategy, as it's like gambling at a casino. You cannot in any way influence what happens or manage risks, as everything depends on good luck.

Technical analysis (TA): TA involves looking at charts of a coin's trading activity, such as price movement and volume, to forecast (sometimes years in advance) whether to buy or sell it. TA has shown some success in evaluating traditional securities, but cryptocurrency is so new and different that many experts believe it's not as useful in forecasting coins. Some people swear by TA (Figure 5.1), but many consider it to be akin to astrology or palm reading.

If you want to learn more about it, you can find various TA guides online. A useful site is TradingView.com, which allows users to create charts and share their TA predictions at no charge. Keep in mind, TA is not something you can become an expert at just watching a short YouTube tutorial. For example, what appears to be a "Doubles Bottom" pattern, which indicates

Figure 5.1 Example of a TA "cup and handle" pattern

you should buy, may turn out to be a "Rectangle Top" pattern, which means you should sell. It takes years of experience and the ability to grasp complex statistical patterns and economic trends to master this method, so it is not user-friendly for new investors. If it was easy to do TA and often worked, everyone would be doing it.

Diversify your portfolio

Whichever investment strategy you choose, portfolio diversification is a must. You might think you've identified an altcoin that's a sure thing and will moon. This might tempt you into investing all your money into this one coin. But such a strategy is extremely risky and often backfires. All kinds of unexpected things can happen that could cause a coin's price to plummet overnight. So, spread your risk and diversify your holdings. To begin with, I'd suggest maybe 40% Bitcoin, 30% Ethereum and 30% altcoins (once you feel ready to invest in altcoins, that is). As you become a more seasoned investor, you might find a formula that works better, or you might want to roll the dice and take more risks. But whatever you do, never put all your eggs in one basket.

Choosing an altcoin exchange

Where should you buy your altcoins? There are dozens of exchanges all over the world that sell altcoins. Choose wisely. Some are much better than others.

Avoid using shady exchanges. How do you know an exchange is untrustworthy? Do a Google search for the exchange's name and see if any news stories or forum threads pop up warning about it. For example, I noticed a coin I wanted to buy was selling much cheaper on YoBit, a Russian exchange, than it was on Cryptopia, a New Zealand exchange. I was obviously tempted to buy the coin on Yobit to save money. But the significant price difference raised a red flag in my head – as I mentioned earlier, if something seems too good to be true it probably is. A quick Google search revealed the exchange was being investigated by authorities for fraud and that many customers complained that they were unable to withdraw the coins they purchased on it.

At the moment, few trustworthy exchanges exist that allow you to buy altcoins with fiat (i.e. money from your bank account). Instead, you'll first need to buy Bitcoin or Ethereum on an exchange such as Coinbase or Gemini and then transfer it to another platform, such as Binance or Bittrex, which sells altcoins in exchange for Bitcoin and Ethereum. When transferring your coins from one wallet or exchange to another, be extra careful.

Mistyping the address where you intend to send your coins could result in your coins being forever lost in cyberspace. So, initially, do a test deposit in which you send a small amount of cryptocurrency to a wallet or exchange to make sure it works OK. (More on wallets later on.)

Placing orders on exchanges

In order to buy altcoins, someone needs to be selling! So once on the exchange, navigate to the order book and see what the going price is for your coin of choice. If you set your buy order (bid) for a higher price than the lowest seller's price (ask), it will typically be filled very quickly. If not, you may need to wait a bit for your order to be filled. Once someone accepts your bid, the order is filled, and that altcoin will be stored in your account within the exchange.

Let's break down how to place orders on the exchange.

There are various ways you can buy and sell on an exchange. All orders fall under two main categories: 1) market orders allow you to buy and sell instantly at whatever price others will accept, and 2) pending orders don't get filled until your specified selling or buying criteria are met. Pending orders can be limit orders, stop orders or stop-limit orders. All of these orders can be used to buy or sell cryptocurrency. Ordering can look a bit different depending on the exchange, but the basic principles are the same.

On cryptocurrency exchanges, the sellers set the price they want to get for their coins, which is known as the "ask." Meanwhile, the buyers give the price that they are willing to pay for coins, which is known as the "bid." The difference between the buy and ask price is the "spread." The spread is bridged through bargaining – the buyer might raise their bid, the seller might lower their ask, or both sides may compromise and meet somewhere in the middle. So, the orders of both the sellers and buyers stand in a kind of line. To be the first in line, you must offer the best price. Each price has an indication of the volume (or amount of coins) the buyer wants to buy, or the seller wants to sell. These lines of pending orders on both the ask and bid side are known as market depth. The graphical representation on the depth chart looks like walls (Figure 5.2).

The easiest way to buy or sell something on an exchange is to place a **market order**. This order is executed at the current market price immediately after placing it on the exchange (assuming someone is selling or buying coins). When making a market order to buy coins, the buyer pays the ask price. When making a market order to sell coins, the seller sells at the bid price. When making a market order, you do not need to specify the price; you only need to specify the volume – i.e. how many coins you want to buy or sell. The price is whatever the best offer is.

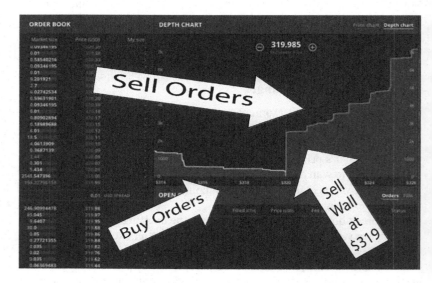

Figure 5.2 This is what an exchange order book looks like

However, there is a big problem you can encounter known as "slippage." Sometimes there's a noticeable difference between the expected price of a trade and the price at which the trade actually executes. Slippage often occurs during periods of higher volatility. It can also occur when there are large orders, if there's insufficient interest at the desired price level to maintain the expected price of the trade. Given this, I do not recommend using market orders.

For example, say you place a market order to purchase 1,000 coins of Cardano when the best offer price is 20 cents per coin. If other orders in the queue are executed before your trade order, your market order may fill at a higher price. You may end up paying 25 cents per coin. It's also possible that portions of your order could execute at different prices. In this example, half of the order might fill at the best offer price (20 cents) and the other half could execute at a higher price (23 cents). A market order does not guarantee getting a certain price; it only guarantees your order will be filled.

To avoid slippage, use a limit order, instead. A **limit order** is an order to buy or sell a certain amount of a cryptocurrency at a specific price. For instance, if you want to buy Cardano at 18 cents, but it is trading at 20 cents, you can set a limit order for 18 cents. This guarantees that you will pay no more than 18 cents to buy each coin. It's possible your order won't fill. Remember, you'll have to wait in the bid line. It may happen that Cardano's price doesn't dip, and your order goes unfilled. Or there could be insufficient coins being sold at your bid price to fully fill your order of 1,000 coins, and you may only end up getting 500 coins at your bid price. In order to ensure your order gets filled, you should evaluate the order book and place your order at a price and volume where it will likely execute instead of at the price you wish it would execute at.

A third type of order to know is a **stop order**. This is an order to buy or sell cryptocurrency when its price surpasses a particular price point. Let's say you're looking to sell your NEO, so you set an exit price of $50 per coin. Once the price reaches $50, your stop order turns into a regular market order. However, I don't recommend using this type of order. Many sellers assume that stop orders will protect them from losses if the price starts to fall, but it often doesn't work that way. Your coins will be automatically sold at the best available price, so many of your coins could end up selling for much less than $50. Another investor (sometimes called a "whale") or coordinated group of investors who own many NEO coins could trigger the stop order by doing a massive sell-off and then quickly buying back their and your coins at a cheaper price. Such market manipulation is not uncommon in cryptocurrency. About 40% of Bitcoin is held by perhaps 1,000 people, according to *Bloomberg Businessweek*.[3]

There is also a stop-limit order, which combines the features of a stop order and limit order. A **stop-limit order** requires setting two price points. The first point initiates the start of the buy or sell, referred to as the stop, while the second point represents the other party's target price, referred to as the limit. I'd also avoid using a stop-limit. It does not guarantee the order execution, even if a price reaches a given stop price because the limit might not work. In addition, not all exchanges offer this type of trade order.

Finally, you can add stipulations to the aforementioned order types known as **"good till cancelled"** (GTC) and **"fill or kill."** A GTC order remains active until you either rescind it or the trade executes. A fill or kill order is a variation of the limit order. If your limit order cannot get fully filled (e.g., you want to buy 100 coins at $1, but only 50 coins are available for that price), your order will be cancelled.

Safely store your cryptocurrency

When you buy cryptocurrency on an exchange, whether it's Coinbase, Binance or some other exchange, it will be stored on the exchange. This is known as a "hot wallet." A hot wallet stores your coins online and is connected in some way to the Internet. Many people store their cryptocurrency on the exchange they bought it on. It's easy and automatic. However, it's not recommended to keep your coins stored on an exchange long-term. (That said, Coinbase seems quite secure. Then again, some users have complained they've had their accounts randomly closed and have been unable to recover their funds!)

Many exchanges have been hacked and account holders often are never compensated for the stolen cryptocurrency because exchanges are not FDIC-insured like banks. You may also have your computer, email or smartphone hacked, which may result in someone gaining access to your exchange login info and transferring all your funds out. Even if you set up two-factor authentication using your smartphone and take other security measures, you could still fall victim to a hacker.

The good news is you have other options besides storing your coins on exchanges. For example, there are "software wallets." These are apps you can download to your smartphone, tablet or computer to store your cryptocurrency on. Many cryptocurrencies develop their own free wallet apps for storing coins. However, these can be a risky way of storing cryptocurrency too. That's because, like exchanges, they are connected to the Internet and can get hacked. You may want to store small amounts of cryptocurrency on an app or hot wallet in order to make payments (as we covered in a previous section, more and more merchants are accepting payments using cryptocurrency), but you probably should not store all of your crypto funds on a hot wallet, such as an app or exchange – at least, that's the prevailing advice of security experts.

So, how do you protect your coins from being stolen? You should look into storing your coins offline until you're ready to sell them. This is known as "cold storage." There are a few options for cold storage. Two popular methods of cold storage are 1) a special device such as a Trezor Hardware Wallet (Figure 5.3) or Ledger Nano and 2) a paper wallet.

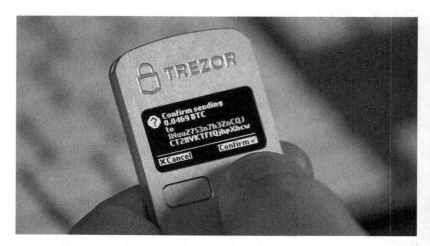

Figure 5.3 An example of a hardware wallet

Source: CC BY-SA Pavol Rusnak

Keep in mind that your coins only exist in cyberspace on the blockchain. There's no way to download your coins and bring them into the physical world. Instead, you will be given what's known as a "private key." This is a randomly generated, very long, alphanumeric password that enables you to access your coins on the blockchain so you can transfer them. It's such a complicated password that it's virtually impossible for anyone to guess or crack. Therefore, your private key(s) should be saved – either on a device like a Trezor or it should be printed on a piece of paper (i.e. a paper wallet). Never share your private key with anyone. If someone knows your private key, that person can steal all your cryptofunds. Also be very careful not to lose your private key because if you do, you will not be able to access your cryptofunds. Those cryptofunds will essentially be unrecoverable. Therefore, you may want to both memorize your private key and create a backup, in case if there's a fire and your cold storage wallet perishes.

Hardware wallets, such as the Trezor or Nano Ledger, can be purchased online for about $100 (be sure to buy a new device from a reputable merchant as a used device may contain malware). Or you can create a free paper wallet using MyEtherWallet.com (a.k.a. MEW).

Don't overlook security

Using proper security measures to protect your cryptocurrency is annoying and time-consuming. That's why many people just keep their coins stored on the exchange. But all it takes is one hack or mistake for you to regret that decision. You might lose everything. So, take the time to properly protect your cryptocurrency. In addition to using cold storage, you should 1) use strong, unique passwords with two-factor authorization for your exchange accounts and 2) install anti-malware software on the devices you use to manage cryptocurrency.

Besides hackers, don't let yourself be your own worst enemy by losing access to your cryptocurrency funds. If you're a forgetful person, you might want to write down your account and wallet information in a notebook and store it in a secure place. Additionally, you may want to take measures to protect posterity. Consider giving written instructions to someone you trust on how to access your cryptocurrency in the event you unexpectedly become indisposed or perish and you're unable to liquidate your investments.

How to sell cryptocurrency

Once your cryptocurrency's price has gone up to a point where you'd be satisfied selling it (or if it's fallen to the point you want to cut your losses and run – it's good to be a realist in crypto), you need to transfer your coins back to an exchange (if they're stored in a wallet or cold storage) and set an "ask" price. When you do this, you can set the price at which you would like your trade to execute. You can sell one coin at a time if you want, but most people do a batch sale, or several partial sales across a certain amount to catch price swings. When a buyer accepts your ask price, your trade will execute, and your account on the exchange will be filled with the buyer's Bitcoin or Ethereum (note: some exchanges also offer other trade pairings. For example, you may be able to convert an altcoin for Litecoin or NEO). From there, you can swap for cash.

Converting crypto back to fiat

Whether you're holding Bitcoin or an altcoin, such as Ripple, here's how you go about converting your cryptocurrency into traditional money.

Not all exchanges allow you to liquidate cryptocurrency (including BTC and ETH) into fiat (such as U.S. dollars and euros). On many popular alt-coin exchanges, such as Binance, you'll first need to convert (sell) your altcoins for Bitcoin or Ethereum. Then you'll need to transfer that Bitcoin or Ethereum to a liquidation-friendly exchange, such as Coinbase, which allows account holders to sell their Bitcoin and Ethereum for U.S. dollars. You can then wire the money to your bank account. Be aware that both the exchanges and your bank likely have fees, so a small fraction of your funds will be deducted to cover those fees.

Another option is a so-called stablecoin such as Tether – although it's risky. Binance, Bittrex and many exchanges allow users to convert coins into Tether. Tether is a controversial token claimed by its creators to be backed by one U.S. dollar for each token issued, though the Tether company has not issued an audit of its currency reserves. When you're ready to jump back into the cryptocurrency market, you can exchange your Tethers for coins. But some experts doubt whether Tether truly has enough funds to cover their liabilities. Tether is also largely unregulated. Tether holders have no contractual rights, other legal claims or guarantees against losses. Given this, some worry that Tether could become insolvent at any time and Tether holders could lose all their funds. In fact, widespread concern over Tether's reliability may have contributed to the cryptocurrency market's recession in 2018.

Aside from these options, there are other ways to convert cryptocurrency to cash, but they are less common, typically complicated and may get you in trouble with law enforcement. So, I won't elaborate on them.

Know when to buy, sell and hold

With 24/7 exchanges that never close (except for occasional website main-tenance and upgrades), you can buy and sell cryptocurrency at any time.

It's natural to want to buy as soon as you login to an exchange and transfer in your funds. But patience often pays off. Given price fluctuations and the market's infamous volatility, there are better times than others to conduct transactions.

When you're just starting out in crypto, you might want to watch a coin for a week or longer before you buy. At the very least, you should look at the coin's and overall market's charts for the past week, month and year to see if it's in a general downtrend (in which case, you might want to wait longer to buy) or uptrend (in which case, you might jump in before the price goes much higher). Doing such research will help you identify a target price for buying your coins.

When it comes to buying, a basic investment strategy is to "buy the dips" (BTD). This doesn't mean going all in while a coin's price is going down; rather, it means average in as it goes down or buy when it settles at a consistent price range. Specifically, that means doing one or more of the following: 1) buying incrementally as the price goes down and buying more as the price decreases further; 2) waiting until the price settles, and perhaps even shows signs of recovering, and buying at that point; 3) setting buy orders at lower prices than the current price and waiting for them to fill.

Of course, timing the bottoms of those dips is next to impossible, and that is why it can help to buy incrementally as the price falls. "It's hard to catch a falling knife," as the saying goes. In crypto, there are many little dips, and then every few weeks or months, there tends to be some very big dips (what are called "corrections" or "crashes"). For example, Bitcoin's market frequently goes through reoccurring cycles that look something like what is shown in Figure 5.4.

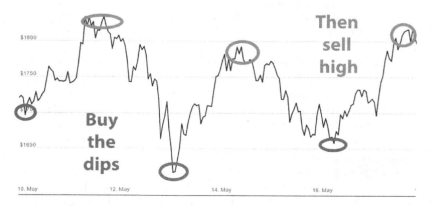

Figure 5.4 An illustration of when to buy and sell

Buying the dip can be psychologically difficult, though. Crypto prognosticators often scream "buy the dip!," but few traders actually do so because, as humans, we're wired to avoid an investment that's been in the red a lot recently.

Another buying strategy is to "dollar cost average" (DCA) your purchase of a coin. You can do this a few ways, but a common approach with dollar cost averaging is to spend the same dollar amount every X amount of time. So, if I had $1,200 to spend, I'd spend $100 a month, every month on the same date, over the period of a year. I would therefore end up with an average price in the coin. As an alternative version of the strategy, you can break your buys up to weekly or daily buys, or aim to buy only on the dips or skip periods when the price has gone up very high. This sort of incremental buying can be effective for building long positions in cryptocurrency due to the volatility of the market.

It's also good to keep some fiat available. This way you can buy if there's a sudden, big price drop. Granted, it's human nature to FOMO into buying a coin as the price goes up and then to become trapped. But don't overextend yourself. Keeping fiat on hand gives you wiggle room. Remember what happened to Bitcoin in December 2017 – its price doubled from $10,000 to $20,000 as many investors FOMO'd in. By February 2018, Bitcoin's price was down to $7,300. If those same December investors had waited a month, they could have purchased Bitcoin for nearly $13,000 less. The lesson: don't try to jump onto a fast-moving train – you'll get hurt badly. Instead, wait for the next stop to get on. If a coin's price has increased significantly in a short period of time, it's due for a correction.

Whatever buying strategy you use, always keep an eye on Bitcoin. If Bitcoin's price pumps parabolically, the price of altcoins typically goes down as people try to exit altcoins to ride the Bitcoin profits. Inversely, if Bitcoin's price drops drastically, altcoin prices usually go down, too, as people exit altcoins to exchange back into fiat. The best times for altcoin growth are when Bitcoin shows slow growth or slow decline or remains stagnant in price.

If you buy a cryptocurrency at a certain price and don't see strong up or down movements, do not fall into panic and sell it immediately. Eventually, most coins with solid fundamentals increase in value, but it might take several months or even years – recall Bitcoin's price history. I know plenty of examples of when the seemingly stable price of a coin suddenly increased tenfold within a week. For example, Tron leapt some 90% in a day after its founder issued a vague tweet about upcoming partnerships.

Sharp price increases are seldom random; they're often prompted by catalysts, such as news of a new exchange listing, a new partnership or release of new product. For example, just getting listed on Binance can temporarily boost a cryptocurrency 80% in market value.[4] You can find info about such developments on the coin's official communication channels (e.g., its blog, Twitter, Telegram) and sites such as Coindar, which lists coins' announcements and upcoming events.

On the other hand, announcements of regulation, security breaches or technical problems can send prices plummeting to the ground. Don't expect a company to share bad news. Instead, you'll need to monitor social and news media for these developments and be prepared to sell quickly if it's really devastating news. Usually, though, your best move is to just sit back and "hodl" (which means hold in crypto slang). Remember, this is an investment (which means investing money now so you can earn profits later), not an instant scratch-off lottery ticket.

Even when the price is on the rise, it won't be nonstop gains. There will be dips. Holding entails weathering those dips and uncertainty. Even during Bitcoin's meteoric rise in 2017 – from $900 to $20,000 – there were periods of significant dips. Another reason you may want to hold long-term is tax benefits. If you hold a particular coin for a year or more, you will pay a lower tax rate (more on this in the superseding chapter on law).

That said, don't hold too long. Know when to sell and take a profit. The most successful gamblers know when to walk away from the table. Don't get greedy. It's easier said than done, of course. As your coin grows in value, so does the greed inside you. But your greed may result in you not only missing out on profits, but suffering a loss, as well. Set realistic profit goals and sell or at least pare down once you hit them. No one ever lost money taking a profit. If a coin increases by 25%, why not consider taking profit? Even if your goal is 50%, you should at least pull out some of the profit on the way up in case the coin doesn't reach your goal.

One popular strategy for selling is known as "laddering." Instead of selling all your coins at a single price, you set incremental sell limit orders at different price points on the order book, selling part of your portfolio when the price goes up. (The laddering strategy can be used for buying, as well.)

You should at least cash out your initial investment as soon as you reasonably can, so that you're left playing with "house money." For example, if you invest $1,000, you might sell and recoup that initial investment once your portfolio hits $2,000. That means you have retained your initial investment and still have $1,000 to play with. Or you might wait until your portfolio hits $5,000 to withdraw your initial investment. But don't get greedy and wait too long to cash out your initial investment. Otherwise, given the routine market fluctuations, there could come a time when you not only lose your profits but also lose much of your initial investment.

Keep in mind that bearish periods (when prices are trending down) usually last much longer than bull runs (when prices are increasing). Sometimes, converting your coins into fiat (traditional money such as U.S. dollars) and sitting out of the cryptocurrency market is your best option. The market can be quite bearish at times, and there's no profit to be made. There are periods when just about every coin is dropping in price, and it's best to keep your money on the sidelines until the market picks up again. Granted, it's difficult to time an ideal entry and exit point.

Try not to get too emotionally attached to your coins. They are just a means to an end: profiting. Put aside the fear that comes when everyone is selling during a dip. You also have to resist the impulse to buy high when it seems everyone is buying. Sure, you'll miss part of the run, or you'll miss your chance to sell at the highest possible price, but you'll be making safer bets a lot of the time if you wait for some confirmation of an uptrend or downtrend. This is generally true, even though you could end up missing some profit-making opportunities this way.

There will likely be a time that you make a great decision or a terrible one to buy, trade or sell. In either case, your emotions will be at a peak, making you vulnerable. When you make a really shrewd trade, you'll feel like a genius. This can lead to you becoming overconfident and starting to get careless and risky with your decisions. On the other hand, if you make a really bad trade, resulting in you down 20% or more on your portfolio, you might try to correct it by making another trade immediately after. This psychological tendency is like the cliché gambler who loses big at the blackjack table. Instead of walking away with a loss, his gut convinces him to play just one more hand and double down his bets in order to recover his losses. Similarly, in cryptocurrency, the mind-set of "I'm just one trade away from fixing that horrible mistake" can take over, which is usually quickly followed by desperation. This leads to disaster. Take the loss and take a break from trading. Everyone loses and experiences bad luck at some point. Don't beat yourself up about it, and definitely don't make an emotional trade soon after to try to make up for it. It will only make matters worse.

Investment opportunities to avoid

In addition to resisting emotional trades, I strongly advise you don't mess with day trading, futures, ICOs, P&D groups or anything like that – at least, not until you're a seasoned investor and willing to take big risks.

Day trading involves the buying and selling of a cryptocurrency within a single trading day. Research shows that about 80% of day traders fail in their first two years.[5] Few people have the education, experience and skills it takes to succeed. It's like sitting your grandma down at her first game of Texas Hold'em and expecting her to clean up – how do you think that would go? Day trading is also a big-time commitment. You can't just hop onto your laptop every few hours poolside between martinis and expect to turn profits. It's a full-time job that requires constantly monitoring news and exchanges all over the world. If you haven't done day trading with traditional assets, such as stocks, in the past, don't start with cryptocurrency.

> You can keep track of your investments using a free app, such as Blockfolio.

Futures (or derivatives) are basically a bet between two parties about the future price of Bitcoin. You can go "long," meaning you expect the price to increase, or bet that prices will fall (known as shorting). BitMEX is a popular exchange for Bitcoin futures. But given Bitcoin's wild price swings and possible price manipulation by whales and collectives, trading futures is a bad idea. Additionally, some nations, such as South Korea, prohibit citizens from futures trading.

Initial coin offerings, or ICOs, are used by new blockchain projects to raise money. While ICOs often give buyers a chance to purchase a new cryptocurrency before it hits exchanges at a discounted rate, most of these projects end up failing before they leave the gate. Some are downright scams and never launch – the founders take the money and run. Sure, lots of money can be made on ICOs, but 80% of the time, you'll lose money, so buyer beware.[6] In fact, ICOs have developed such a bad reputation that many nations, including the United States, now heavily restrict their citizens from investing. (That said, if you're intent on investing in ICOs and permitted to, I offer some guidance in the chapter on "Other topics.")

Definitely stay clear of P&D groups. The P&D is a long-standing practice to quickly raise the value of a worthless asset and then immediately sell it to reap the profits from the price increase. In the traditional investment world such as the stock market, P&D schemes are illegal. But because of a lack of regulation in the cryptocurrency space, it happens quite frequently. It's unethical and very risky. These groups are sometimes advertised on social media, and they move very fast. The runners drop their coin call, and by the time you can log onto the exchange, it is already up 20% with volume increasing sharply. Obviously, the runners preset their sell target just below the target for the group to guarantee their profits. Some people make a nice profit, but many more lose money or get stuck "hodling" and hoping.

Cryptocurrency is still like the Old Wild West, with lots of scams, insider trading and other dangers, and you open yourself up to more risks by day trading, playing futures, participating in P&D groups and investing in ICOs.

Obey the law

Remember: cryptocurrency gains are subject to taxes in most countries. Under U.S. law, for example, if you hold your investment for less than one year before selling for fiat or trading for another coin, you will have to pay a higher capital gains tax rate than if you hold long term. This means day trading can get very messy when it comes to taxes. Keep accurate records of all your cryptocurrency transactions – e.g., how much fiat you invested, which trades you made, how much you lost or profited from each trade and/or how much you converted back to fiat. You'll need all of this info to ensure that you properly report and pay the taxes you owe. If you lose money investing, you may be able to partially write off the losses.

Record keeping is your responsibility; exchanges will not send you a tax form such as a 1099 detailing your transactions. Consult a lawyer or accountant if you have questions. Fines and penalties may be steep if you don't honestly and accurately report your holdings and returns. The Internal Revenue Service (IRS) is starting to get very serious about cracking down on cryptocurrency tax evaders.

More information on taxes will be provided in a later section covering cryptocurrency laws.

Closing advice

What I've provided in this chapter is a set of basic guidelines to follow to invest in cryptocurrency. But that doesn't mean you shouldn't experiment on your own – and sometimes that experimentation means breaking some of the "rules" I've set forth here. Sometimes taking risks pays off. You might identify a better strategy for finding crypto's next hidden gem. Don't feel limited by what you read in this book. Feel empowered to know what works most of the time, but that some of the time it doesn't.

You're probably going to suffer through some growing pains before becoming successful. You will make mistakes. You may buy a coin only to see it immediately decline in price and continue to for a long period. Or you may sell a coin and then lament when you see it increase tenfold over the following week.

As Aziz Zainuddin, founder of MasterTheCrypto.com, explains,

> Everyone loses money trading, that's just a part of the game. Even the experts lose money. If they claim that they don't, then they're

simply lying to you. It's hard if not downright impossible to get every call right. There's just some shit that's not going to go your way and there's nothing you'll really be able to do about it. In those cases, you have to be able to accept your losses and move on. . . . Michael Jordan never won every game that he ever played. In fact, he's lost hundreds if we're counting the regular season. He's lost playoff games and championship ones too. Going undefeated isn't what makes you great, it's being a consistent winner overall. It's okay to take a loss as long as you're in net profit. That's the mark that you should aim to hit.[7]

Don't let the losses discourage you because they can help make you better trader if you choose to learn from them. Figure out what went wrong and apply that knowledge to your next move, which should be better because you'll know more than you knew before. There are many tragic tales about traders who had great success only to lose it all later. Hopefully, you won't end up like that because you'll be practicing the smart investment techniques you learned in this book. However, it is a possibility if you don't educate yourself and remain disciplined in this volatile and risky market.

Guide to altcoins

The following is a brief description of ten of the most popular alternative cryptocurrencies to Bitcoin and Ethereum.

Cryptocurrency (Trading Symbol)	Summary
Litecoin (LTC)	Litecoin is basically a faster version of Bitcoin, with Litecoin transactions taking just over 2 minutes to go through in comparison to Bitcoin's 28 minutes. Litecoin was one of the first altcoins, created in 2011 by Charlie Lee, a former Google employee, who was unsatisfied with the long confirmation wait times of Bitcoin transactions. He created Litecoin from a copy of Bitcoin's open-source code and then modified it to include aspects which he felt were lacking in Bitcoin. Litecoin is four times faster than Bitcoin and has transaction fees that are only a fraction of Bitcoin's. Because of this, Litecoin is much better for making small transactions; transaction speed and fees are top concerns

(*Continued*)

Cryptocurrency (Trading Symbol)	Summary
	for cryptocurrency users. Litecoin is accepted by almost as many merchants as Bitcoin. Litecoin's coin supply is 84 million, which is four times as many coins as Bitcoin's total supply. Like Bitcoin, it's a mineable coin; however, Litecoin is easier for individuals to mine because its software uses a different algorithm. Lee sold nearly all of his Litecoin holdings in December 2017, when LTC was at its peak price at about $375, leading to controversy and criticism from the LTC community. Lee, however, continues to work full time with the Litecoin Foundation to promote adoption of the coin. This gives it an advantage over Bitcoin, whose founder disappeared years ago. Following the market-wide recession, Litecoin was selling for about $31 per coin in December 2018. Most popular exchanges offer LTC trading and it ranks in the top-ten of cryptocurrencies in terms of marketcap. You can buy it with fiat on Coinbase.
Monero (XMR)	Monero is widely regarded as the preeminent "privacy coin" in cryptocurrency. It was created in 2014 as a fork of the cryptocurrency Bytecoin. There are about 16.5 million coins in circulation, but, unlike Bitcoin, Monero does not have a hard maximum cap in order to ensure that coins will be available to incentivize miners to maintain the blockchain indefinitely. In further contrast to Bitcoin, which makes its transaction details viewable on a public ledger, Monero uses ring signature cryptography to hide much information about transactions from public view. While anybody can broadcast or send transactions, no outside observer can see the source, amount or destination. While this makes it the cryptocurrency of choice for many criminals, there are also good reasons why a law-abiding person may want to use Monero. After the string of security breaches over the past few years that have leaked credit card data, financial privacy has become very important. Additionally, with Visa, PayPal and other payment platforms refusing to do business with certain politically controversial causes and people (such as WikiLeaks), alternative, anonymous transaction methods have become necessary. Monero's technology isn't entirely foolproof, however, and some issues still need to be worked out to ensure complete anonymity. It has a strong and dedicated development team, led by Riccardo Spagni, that regularly updates its product. Monero was the best-performing cryptocurrency in 2016, with nearly a 3,000% increase. It achieved an all-time high of about $540 during cryptocurrency's boom in 2017–2018 but sold for about $60 in December 2018. It ranks in the top ten of cryptocurrencies for marketcap. You can buy it on many exchanges, including Binance, but not Coinbase.

Cryptocurrency (Trading Symbol)	Summary
Ripple (XRP)	If you spend any time in cryptocurrency circles, the coin Ripple is bound to come up in conversation. The crypto world has a love-hate relationship with Ripple. While cryptocurrency purists despise it, it represents an intriguing investment opportunity. Ripple markets itself as a cross-border payments solution for major banks based on blockchain technology. Backed by Google and several banks, this controversial cryptocurrency took the market by storm in 2017–2018, spiking in price from less than a penny to nearly $4 per coin during a one-year span. For brief periods, Ripple has surpassed Ethereum in market capitalization and become the No. 2 ranked cryptocurrency behind only Bitcoin. As of December 2018, following a year-long, market-wide recession, Ripple had dropped to about 40 cents per coin. But it continues to be a hot topic and has generated tremendous buzz in the mainstream media and debate on social media. In short, many experts don't consider Ripple to be a "real cryptocurrency" because it utilizes a centralized blockchain. Its network is completely controlled by the Ripple company. This means that the company has the power to devalue it, increase its coin supply (despite saying it won't) and change the blockchain – all of which concerns cryptocurrency enthusiasts. Additionally, mining and forging are not possible. Ripple officials counter that the coin's centralization makes it more stable and reliable than other cryptocurrencies. And it's established many enviable partnerships. Ultimately, Ripple could go either way: it might be a game-changer or fail spectacularly. As of December 2018, Ripple was worth about 40 cents and ranked in the top-three coins among cryptocurrency marketcaps. Despite long denying it would add Ripple to its exchange, Coinbase ultimately added the cryptocurrency in 2019.
Cardano (ADA)	Cardano is a third-generation blockchain platform that seeks to improve on Bitcoin (1st generation) and Ethereum (2nd) and create a blockchain technology that can support an online ecosystem of apps, smart contracts, monetary transactions and more. Right now, neither Bitcoin nor Ethereum can process transactions fast enough to support a large endeavor such as a social network or financial market. Facebook alone pumps out 52,000 likes per second, and many more posts and messages. In order for Facebook to run just one component of its network on blockchain technology, a platform like Ethereum would need to be $10,000\times$ more efficient than it currently is.

(*Continued*)

Cryptocurrency (Trading Symbol)	Summary
	Cardano hopes to change that by implementing two upgrades called "Sharding" and "Plasma," which would allow faster, cheaper and more scalable transactions. It's still very much a work in progress, but Cardano's potential has enabled it to achieve a top-ten ranking among cryptocurrencies, in terms of marketcap. However, because Cardano has such a large coin supply like Ripple, individual coins have only achieved an all-time high value of about $1. Like Ethereum and NEO, Cardano allows for the creation of new tokens and decentralized applications, therefore creating an inherent value similar to ETH in its ability to provide infrastructure for other tokens and DApps its network. Cardano offers the ability to stake coins – essentially the chance to earn interest on your holdings. It does not rely entirely on voluntary and often unfunded development, but instead has a fully funded development team, Input Output Hong Kong. It was created by Charles Hoskinson, a co-founder of the Ethereum project, but it hopes to someday overtake Ethereum in marketcap value. Cardano is available on Binance and could soon be added to Coinbase.
Eosio (EOS)	Launched in 2017, EOS is the latest project by accomplished blockchain entrepreneur Dan Larimer (who also created BitShares, STEEM and BitUSD). Larimer is head of Block.one, a Cayman Islands-based blockchain company that's developing the EOS platform. Like Cardano, it's one of several cryptocurrency projects attempting to build a next generation blockchain that becomes superior to Bitcoin and Ethereum by improving scalability. Like ETH and Cardano, EOS is a platform that can support tokens, smart contracts and DApps. EOS has ambitious goals: it basically wants to create an online operating system that can support industrial-scale decentralized applications, such as a major social network, and serve millions of people, which no blockchain is currently capable of. Consider that Ethereum's network at one point in 2017 nearly came to a standstill due to the bandwidth required to run a suddenly popular cat-trading game known as "CryptoKitties." An estimated 30,000 transactions became stuck in the verification process and some users had to wait 20+ hours for their confirmations to go through, CoinDesk reported.[8] EOS aims to blow its competition away by completely removing transaction fees and having the ability to conduct millions of transactions per second. If EOS can deliver – and, right now, that's a big if – it will be a major game-changer. The hype alone, though, enabled EOS to enjoy rapid growth in 2018 despite the

Cryptocurrency (Trading Symbol)	Summary
	market downturn. EOS hit an ATH of about $23 in late April 2018 and sold for about $3.50 per coin in December 2018, which ranks it in the top five of cryptocurrency marketcaps. EOS is not mineable, relying instead on PoS, and has a coin supply of about one billion. It's available on many exchanges, including Binance.
NEO (NEO)	The term "neo" means new or modified, making this cryptocurrency aptly named because it was rebranded from its original name, Antshares. Founded in 2014 by Da Hongfei, NEO is the first major cryptocurrency launched in China and is aiming for a similar goal as the Ethereum project. In fact, it's often referred to as the "Chinese Ethereum." It's a blockchain platform that supports smart contracts, DApps and tokens. Because NEO supports several coding languages, it arguably has an advantage over Ethereum, which requires developers to learn its unique code before they can use the platform to create smart contracts, tokens and DApps. Unlike most cryptocurrencies, NEO is not mineable and it's largely centralized. A Chinese company known as OnChain funded its development and continues to control it. NEO will never generate more coins than its existing 100 million – in theory – and trades only in whole units – not in fractions, like other cryptocurrencies. NEO holders regularly receive a token known as GAS, which acts as fuel for the NEO blockchain to run DApps and smart contracts, and provides incentives for maintaining the blockchain. The dividend is proportional to how much NEO they own. It means that NEO consistently produces value that can be sold without losing the initial stake. NEO is tacitly backed by the Chinese government, making it resilient to cryptocurrency legal uncertainty inside China and giving it a huge advantage in attracting partnerships and adoption in China. NEO peaked at about $200 in January 2018 but had fallen below $10 in December 2018. Still, it ranked among the top 20 cryptocurrencies in marketcap. Buying NEO directly from fiat is a little difficult, but many exchanges, including Binance, allow you to exchange BTC or ETH for NEO.
Stellar Lumens (XLM)	Stellar Lumens is a cryptocurrency platform that wants to become a better version of PayPal. Its goal is to make monetary transactions that are quicker, cheaper and more reliable for the average person than they are under current systems. The Stellar network can quickly exchange government-based currencies using its cryptocurrency, Lumens, as a go-between broker. Currently, it can handle 1,000 transactions per second without breaking a sweat and transfer millions of dollars for a few pennies.

(Continued)

Cryptocurrency (Trading Symbol)	Summary
	This is particularly useful for people and businesses in the developing economies, which sometimes have trouble converting their government's currency to other countries' currencies. Stellar is very similar to Ripple, but has some notable differences: it's decentralized, and it aims to be utilized by individuals and small businesses rather than large banks. In that sense, it has a mission with a higher purpose than just replacing hard currency or as investments. Its goal is to connect people to low-cost financial services, which will help everyone and especially the billions of people without bank accounts in the developing world. Stellar allows people to freely send money internationally without the hassle of banks or currency exchange. It has already had much success in Africa and the Mideast and has partnerships with IBM, Deloitte and Stripe, among other prominent companies. The Stellar team functions as a nonprofit organization and is highly regarded in the crypto world. It's led by founder Jed McCaleb (who also founded Ripple and the first major Bitcoin exchange, Mt.Gox). In contrast to most of cryptocurrencies, it has weathered the 2018 market downtown much better. Stellar sold for about 16 cents per coin as of December 2018 and ranked in the top ten of marketcap. It had an all-time high of about $1. With 18 billion coins in circulation and a total supply of 104 billion coins, it has one of the largest coin supplies and will never approach the per coin price of Bitcoin or Ethereum. Stellar is available on Binance and was among a handful of cryptocurrencies that Coinbase added in 2019.
Bitcoin Cash (BCH)	As Bitcoin became more popular, with that popularity arose a series of problems. The network became bogged down by the number of people using it. Consequently, transactions became slower and more costly. Bitcoin's community was split over how to fix these issues. This led to a "hard fork" on August 1, 2017, which gave birth to Bitcoin Cash. Holders of Bitcoin received an equal amount of the new Bitcoin Cash coin. In most respects, Bitcoin Cash is exactly like Bitcoin. You can use it to buy and sell things, it works in much the same way, and it even has the same blockchain history – until August 2017. But there are some notable differences: BCH is faster, has lower transaction fees and is supported by an entirely different team of developers. Roger Ver, an early Bitcoin investor, cryptocurrency entrepreneur and ex-convict, is the de facto spokesman for Bitcoin Cash.

Cryptocurrency (Trading Symbol)	Summary
	The coin's mission is to increase the number of transactions that can be processed by its blockchain network to compete with the volume of transactions that industry giants like Visa and PayPal can currently process – but it's still got a way to go in developing its tech to accomplish that. Bitcoin Cash was quickly adopted by investors, as within 24 hours of its existence it ranked behind only Bitcoin and Ethereum in terms of marketcap. To many people, Bitcoin Cash became a remedy to everything that was wrong with the original Bitcoin, and day by day it keeps attracting new followers. That said, Bitcoin Cash has always been significantly lower in value compared to the original Bitcoin (a.k.a. Bitcoin Core) – that's because Bitcoin enjoys a great advantage as the first and best-known cryptocurrency. Nonetheless, Bitcoin Cash is quite valuable. As of December 2018, BCH had a value of about $180, down from an all-time high of nearly $3,800, and ranks in the top-five cryptocurrencies for marketcap. It's available on Coinbase.
Basic Attention Token (BAT)	In contrast to cryptocurrencies such as EOS and Cardano, which are attempting create a platform that can revolutionize the Internet, BAT is focused on revolutionizing one industry: advertising. Unlike the aforementioned cryptocurrencies on this list, BAT is a utility token and not a coin. As such, it operates on the Ethereum blockchain rather than hosting its own blockchain. BAT is focused on online advertising because it believes the current model is broken: most Internet users utilize ad blockers or ignore ads and advertisers waste money on middlemen, such as third-party ad sellers and tracking services. Here's how BAT plans to improve the experience: advertisers use BAT tokens to purchase advertising space and user views through BAT's digital advertising platform; publishers and content creators (such as websites, bloggers and YouTubers) then receive ad revenue and user contributions in BAT tokens; meanwhile, users can earn BAT tokens for any ads in the BAT platform they see ("ad revenue sharing"). BAT is already integrated with Brave, a new web browser that provides more privacy than Chrome, Safari and other popular browsers. In fact, soon you will be able to earn BAT just by using Brave (although it was not available as of late 2018). BAT hopes to eventually expand to other browsers and websites as well. In addition to purchasing subscriptions to websites and content creators (such as online newspapers and YouTube Red), BAT plans to make their token redeemable for gift cards, discounts and digital goods.

(*Continued*)

(Continued)

Cryptocurrency (Trading Symbol)	Summary
	Even if BAT is able to capture just a fraction of the multi-billion-dollar online advertising market, it will be very lucrative. Launched in 2018, BAT is led by a team of accomplished developers. It was founded by the creator of JavaScript and former co-founder of Mozilla, Brendan Eich. BAT is available on Binance and Coinbase. It currently ranks in the top 50 of marketcaps, selling for about 15 cents per token. It had an ATH of about 95 cents but lost much of its value during the market downturn. However, BAT could pump very quickly and easily surpass its ATH once the market recession ends.
Binance Coin (BNB)	Binance Coin is a token issued by Binance, the world's biggest cryptocurrency exchange. Launched in 2017, it was the brainchild of Binance CEO Changpeng "CZ" Zhao, one of the richest and most enterprising people in the crypto world. BNB token holders can get cheaper trades and other perks within the Binance exchange, so it works as a loyalty program as well as a stand-alone cryptocurrency. Binance is one of the fastest and most-respected crypto exchanges, with over 150 coins listed and nearly $1.5 billion in crypto traded daily. Binance charges a 0.1% fee for crypto trades but provides a 25% discount to users who pay transaction fees using its proprietary Binance Coin. BNB currently operates on the Ethereum blockchain, although this may change in the future if Binance follows through with its plan to develop its own blockchain which will be used to transfer or trade different blockchain assets (in which case BNB will be used to fuel transactions on the Binance Chain). BNB can also be used to fund ICOs for new blockchain startups launched under Binance's incubator. As cryptocurrency and Binance continue to grow in popularity, Binance Coin could become a smart investment. There are currently approximately 100 million BNB tokens; however, Binance does regular coin burns, which decrease that supply. As of December 2018, BNB ranked in the top 15 of cryptocurrency marketcaps and sold for about $5 per coin, down from an all-time high of about $24 during January 2018's bull period. It's available on Binance, of course, along with some other exchanges.

Notes

1 Vitalik Buterin, tweet via @VitalikButerin account, *Twitter* (Feb. 17, 2018), available at https://twitter.com/VitalikButerin/status/964838207215955969.
2 Kai Sedgwick, "Four Cryptocurrencies That Actually Meet the Definition of Vaporware," *Bitcoin.com* (Jan. 8, 2018), available at https://news.bitcoin.com/

tron-cardano-verge-and-ripple-four-cryptocurrencies-that-actually-meet-the-def inition-of-vaporware/.

3 Olga Kharif, "The Bitcoin Whales: 1,000 People Who Own 40 Percent of the Market," *Bloomberg Businessweek* (Dec. 8, 2017), www.bloomberg.com/news/ articles/2017-12-08/the-bitcoin-whales-1-000-people-who-own-40-percent-of-the-market.

4 Brian Penny, "What Is Binance Coin? Introduction to BNB Token," *Crypto Briefing* (Aug. 9, 2018), available at https://cryptobriefing.com/what-is-binance-coin-introduction-to-bnb-token/.

5 Brad M. Barber, Yong-Ill Lee, et al., "Do Day Traders Rationally Learn about Their Ability?" *SSRN Electronic Journal* (Jan. 2014), available at https://faculty. haas.berkeley.edu/odean/papers/Day%20Traders/Day%20Trading%20and%20 Learning%20110217.pdf.

6 Sherwin Dowlat, "ICO Quality: Development & Trading," *Satis Group* (Mar. 21, 2018), available at https://medium.com/satis-group/ico-quality-development-trading-e4fef28df04f.

7 Aziz Zainuddin, "Crypto Trading Guide: 4 Common Pitfalls Every Crypto Trader Will Experience," *Master the Crypto* (Mar. 15, 2018), available at http://staging. masterthecrypto.com/4-common-pitfalls-every-crypto-trader-experience/.

8 Alyssa Hertig, "Cat Fight? Ethereum Users Clash over CryptoKitties," *Coin Desk* (Dec. 7, 2017), available at www.coindesk.com/cat-fight-ethereum-users-clash-cryptokitties-congestion.

6   Legal issues

Although cryptocurrencies such as Bitcoin are often likened to the Old Wild West, that does not mean there aren't any laws governing them. While many issues surrounding the decade-old digital asset remain unclear or unregulated, there are some practices that can get the average retail investor (like yourself) in trouble. For example, most countries tax cryptocurrencies and many nations restrict participation in ICOs. More regulations are likely – and that could be a good or bad thing, depending on who you ask.

> **Cryptocurrency is often likened to the Old Wild West, but just because it's a new technology does not mean there are not any laws.**

This chapter provides a plain-language primer on the most common legal issues that investors need to be aware of and what the future may hold. Cybercrime, privacy, ICO, exchange regulations, terms of service, blockchain governance and proposed regulations are all covered along with a comparison of laws in Asia, Europe and the United States.

Privacy

Online privacy is a paramount concern these days and happens to be one of cryptocurrency's greatest strengths. Its transactions can provide more privacy than traditional payment methods, such as checks or credit cards because it's possible to send and receive cryptocurrency without giving any personally identifying information. But there are limits to this privacy. Transactions are not completely anonymous; rather, they're pseudonymous. Sending and receiving cryptocurrency is like writing books under a pseudonym. You can preserve privacy as long as the pseudonym is not linked to your real identity. In cryptocurrency, your nom de plume is a random alphanumeric like 1Ez49SnczcmAmQX5WpEzKMTdcGF2gpNQ22.

If your address is ever linked to your identity, every transaction will be linked to you because every transaction involving that address is stored forever in the blockchain. As long as you're careful with whom you share both your identity and address with, you probably do not have to worry about your transaction history being publicly exposed. Steps can be taken to strengthen privacy, including using encryption software such as Tor or a VPN and generating a new cryptocurrency address for each transaction.

However, no matter what precautions you take, it's difficult to hide from the government. There are many ways authorities can associate a cryptocurrency address with your identity: registering for an exchange, buying products that are sent to a physical address or using your home Wi-Fi are just a few means. All of this information can be subpoenaed by law enforcement. Although criminals continue to develop sophisticated means to hide their trail when using cryptocurrency, cybersecurity researchers warn that no method is bulletproof.

Law enforcement likely has the forensic tools necessary to uncover your identity if they're motivated to. For instance, Ross Ulbricht, the founder of Silk Road, an online marketplace that sold drugs for Bitcoin, was convicted in 2015 after American law enforcement agents tracked his IP address to an Internet cafe and caught him in the act of logging into the website. More recently, in July 2018, U.S. authorities were able to trace Bitcoin payments allegedly made to Russian agents for meddling in the 2016 U.S. presidential election. In August 2018, Chinese police arrested three hackers who stole nearly $87 million in cryptocurrency. These cautionary tales show what can happen if you use cryptocurrency to engage in illegal activities, such as purchasing contraband online, hacking or tax evasion.

Taxes

Speaking of taxes, yes, you typically must pay them on your cryptocurrency riches, unfortunately. Most countries impose some sort of tax on cryptocurrency, such as a sales tax, income tax or capital gains tax. For example, in the United States, the IRS treats cryptocurrency as property, which subjects it to the same tax regulations as other property investments.

Even in the virtual world of cryptocurrency, nothing can be said to be certain, except death and taxes.

Exchanging cryptocurrency for money, trading cryptocurrency for other cryptocurrency and spending cryptocurrency are all taxable. It does not matter if you sold your Bitcoin for cash, exchanged it for another cryptocurrency or used it to buy a cappuccino. In all three cases, the IRS views it as if you sold the coins. This can create quite a hassle if you're a cryptocurrency day trader because you must report every transaction and calculate the gain or a loss at the point of each transaction.

If you own a particular cryptocurrency for less than a year, you pay the short-term capital gains tax, a tax rate that is identical to your marginal tax rate. If you hold on to your cryptocurrency for a year or more, you qualify for a lower long-term capital gains rate. Any time you sell, trade or buy something with your cryptocurrencies, it resets the counter for long-term capital gains.

Therefore, it's critical to keep accurate records of all your cryptocurrency transactions – e.g., how much money you invested, which trades you made, how much you lost or profited from each trade, how much you converted back to money or spent on purchases. You will need all of this info to ensure that you properly report and pay any taxes you owe. Record keeping is your responsibility; exchanges typically do not send you a 1099 detailing your transactions. Penalties may be steep if you do not honestly and accurately report your holdings and returns.

You're still liable for taxes, even if you do not have the money to show for it. For example, suppose you purchase Ethereum for $600, it appreciates to $630, and then you trade it for $630 worth of Litecoin. That trade is a taxable event, and you owe taxes for the $30 profit you made even if you did not cash it out for fiat. Under 2017 tax reform laws enacted by Congress, swapping one cryptocurrency for another is no longer considered a like-kind exchange. Additionally, if you receive free cryptocurrency through a gift or giveaway – such as a fork or airdrop – that is considered a taxable event too.

The good news is, you only have to pay taxes if you make gains. If you lose money investing, you can at least partially write off the losses. If some of your transactions make profits while others lose money, you simply subtract your losses from your gains and pay taxes on the net profit. If, overall, your losses exceed your gains, you may deduct up to $3,000 per year from your taxable income. Any loss beyond $3,000 may be carried forward, year after year, and deducted until the debt is eliminated. In addition to investment losses, any commission and fees you incur from trading cryptocurrency may be deductible.

If you're living outside America, check with an accountant to see what the specific tax policies are for your jurisdiction. Only a handful countries do not tax cryptocurrency, including Germany (if the investment is held for more than a year); Singapore (if a long-term retail investor); Slovenia (for long-term retail investments); Portugal (for any profits made on cryptocurrency, including short-term investments, such as day trades); and Belarus (which placed a moratorium on cryptocurrency taxes until 2023).

Initial coin offerings

Besides taxes, another big issue investors should research is ICOs, which more and more governments are beginning to regulate. Blockchain projects frequently raise funds by offering a presale on their cryptocurrency before it hits exchanges. But citizens in many nations are effectively barred from investing in these kickstarters. For example, China completely bans ICOs. Meanwhile, ICOs are subjected to heavy regulations in the United States, European Union, Australia, Russia, India, Singapore and Thailand, among other nations. Only certain investors may invest and only if they and the ICO meet certain conditions.

> **Eighty-one percent of ICOs launched since early 2017 have been found to be scams.**

For example, in America, the U.S. Securities and Exchange Commission (SEC) typically considers ICOs to be securities – a tradable financial asset – which subjects them to more regulation. (Oddly, cryptocurrency is not considered a security at the time of this writing, although that could change.) Under an SEC policy adopted in 2017, only an elite, wealthy group of Americans known as "accredited investors" can participate in ICOs. Rather than register with the SEC and deal with its tricky regulations, however, many blockchain projects opt to bar all Americans from investing in their ICO.

Strict regulations like those of the United States have been criticized for putting savvy investors at a disadvantage compared to other nations where no ICO restrictions exist. Some ICOs have gone on to become very profitable cryptocurrencies and early investors reaped tremendous rewards. But U.S. officials maintain their policy is intended to mitigate risk to investors and protect investors from fraud. According to a study by Satis Group, a staggering 81% of ICOs launched since early 2017 have been found to be scams, while only 8% went on to trade on an exchange.[1] Fraudulent ICOs are such a problem that the SEC created a deceptive ICO website, www.howeycoins.com, to educate would-be investors. On the other hand, several governments have opted to leave ICOs largely or completely unregulated, including Canada, South Korea, Japan, Hong Kong and most Caribbean nations.

Exchange regulations

In addition to exercising caution with ICOs, investors should be careful where they buy cryptocurrency. "Many platforms refer to themselves as 'exchanges,' which can give the misimpression to investors that they are regulated or meet the regulatory standards of a national securities exchange," the SEC warned in a statement.[2] Many platforms that sell cryptocurrency are subject to little, if any, government oversight and can do whatever they want with your money.

For example, BitMEX is based in the Republic of Seychelles, where it faces little oversight. Meanwhile, Binance relocated from China to Malta, where cryptocurrency regulations are lax. This isn't to suggest that these exchanges can't be trusted, but rather to make investors aware that they may have no legal recourse if a problem arises.

There are some exceptions. For example, popular American exchanges Coinbase and Gemini are both registered with and regulated by government agencies in the United States. South Korea–based exchanges, such as UPbit and Bithumb and New Zealand–based Cryptopia are also subject to strict regulations by their respective governments.

However, for the most part, it's buyer beware when using most cryptocurrency exchanges. Government officials in your home country do not review the trading protocols used by platforms operating outside their jurisdiction. Sketchy business practices are common. Some exchanges utilize questionable tactics to manipulate prices and profit off of transactions, according to tech blog TechCrunch. For example, if you submit a limit order, you trust the exchange to strictly follow your order, but it may not. Some exchanges use bots that trade coins with themselves to artificially inflate market demand, driving up prices.

Choose your exchange wisely. Before using a new exchange, do a Google search and see if any news stories or forum threads pop up warning about it. A quick search for YoBit at this time of writing, for instance, revealed the Russian exchange is being investigated by authorities for fraud and listed many complaints on online forums from users who allege they're unable to withdraw cryptocurrency they purchased on it.

Cybercrime

ICOs and exchanges are just some of the ways you can be defrauded. If you invest in cryptocurrency, you're certainly in the cross hairs of cybercriminals. According to a 2017 study by Norton Cyber Security, more than half of adults in America and globally said they were the victim of a cybercrime on their home computer in the past year.[3] Your guard should be raised when it comes to cryptocurrency. Hacking and scams are especially rampant in this part of the Internet (Figure 6.1).

A cryptocurrency exchange is hacked seemingly every month. According to the *Wall Street Journal*, nearly $1 billion worth of cryptocurrency was stolen by hackers during the first half of 2018.[4] Unlike U.S. banks, cryptocurrency exchanges are not FDIC-insured, so you might not be reimbursed if the exchange has its coins stolen. Meanwhile, Twitter has been overtaken with accounts impersonating notable figures and businesses promising

Figure 6.1 An example of a popular cryptocurrency scam on social media

Source: Shahzad Afzal

thousands of Bitcoins or Ethereums in return for users merely sending a small amount of a cryptocurrency to their accounts.

Law enforcement is aggressively fighting back. The U.S. government can potentially charge cryptocurrency-related crimes under at least 40 different federal statutes and there are also a number of traditional criminal statutes that apply to such crimes. Several agencies, including the SEC, Federal Bureau of Investigation, Department of Justice, Treasury Department's Financial Crimes Enforcement Network, Federal Trade Commission and Commodity Futures Trading Commission, help enforce the laws. Meanwhile, overseas, INTERPOL, an organization that facilitates police cooperation among its 194 member nations, has created a DarkNet and Cryptocurrencies Working Group to deal with threats. However, catching cryptocurrency criminals is not always easy for a variety of reasons.

Lack of information sharing among law enforcement agencies and limited technological resources and experience among local and developing nation enforcement agencies can make it difficult to uncover a criminal's true identity and prosecute him. "Cryptocurrencies have actually led to a massive cat and mouse game with law enforcement, as agencies get better at identifying criminal behavior, while criminals come up with new evasion techniques and increasingly anonymous cybercurrencies in order to defeat the efforts of law enforcement," IT industry analyst Jason Bloomberg wrote in *Forbes*.[5]

In some cases, laws are murky, enabling exploitation. For example, online gambling involving money is illegal in most states in America. But some online casinos use Bitcoin to skirt around these bans because it's not considered a currency under IRS regulations. Meanwhile, P&D trading schemes are common on exchanges, but not explicitly forbidden. This happens when a group of investors coordinates a massive buy and sell-off a particular cryptocurrency on a particular exchange. Some people make some profit, but many lose money or get left holding the bag. In the traditional investment world such as the stock market, P&D schemes are illegal. But because cryptocurrencies are not considered securities, it's not officially illegal and happens quite frequently. Special legislation may be needed to close these kinds of loopholes.

Cryptocurrency protocols also present barriers for righting wrongs. To prevent double spending, a transaction cannot be reversed by anyone. If something goes wrong with a transaction, there is no way to recover it. There is no safety net to protect you like there is when you use banks or credit cards.

Finally, there are jurisdictional challenges. Cryptocurrency is a global marketplace and no one country controls it. There is no international body that regulates cryptocurrency or global agreement on how it should be governed. Each nation makes its own laws and conflicts often emerge. An investor may reside in America, buy cryptocurrency from an exchange located in Malta and use it to purchase a product from someone in China. If a dispute arises as a result of that chain of transactions, whose laws apply? You could find yourself facing legal claims for activities that are legal in your own country. Or, if you're harmed by a hack or scam involving an overseas transaction, redress may not be available.

Given all these dangers, investors need to protect themselves online. Taking security measures such as using strong passwords with two-factor authentication, installing anti-malware software on devices and storing cryptocurrency offline are essential. At the same time, don't be gaslit by negative media stories. Cryptocurrency arguably has an outsized reputation as being something that is only used for illegal activities.

Although Bitcoin initially gained demand thanks to Silk Road, it's now regarded as a legitimate investment. A 2018 study by the Foundation for Defense of Democracies found that only 1% of all Bitcoin is used for illegal transactions.[6] "Yes it is true that criminals have used Bitcoin, but it is also true that criminals have used airplanes, computers and automobiles," explained Norbert Michel, director for the Center for Data Analysis at the Heritage Foundation, at a congressional hearing. "We should not criminalize any of those instruments simply because criminals used them."[7]

Website terms of use

Governments aren't the only entities that can impose rules affecting the cryptospace. Online businesses offering products and services related to cryptocurrency often have their own sets of terms you must obey if you want to utilize them. Thus, it's important to read the fine print before clicking on a website's or app's terms of use. You could get banned for all kinds of arbitrary reasons.

For example, when Gab announced its Coinbase account was abruptly closed in June 2018, some observers speculated it was because the controversial social media platform may have violated the exchange's user agreement, which prohibits users who "promote, or encourage hate [and] racial intolerance."[8]

Blockchain companies are notorious for banning users from their social media groups if they post negative comments. It's perfectly legal too. America may be known as a bastion for free speech, but the First Amendment of its Constitution prohibits only the government from censoring citizens. Private businesses aren't obligated to provide free speech; however, critics argue that censorship violates cryptocurrency's spirit.

Blockchain governance

Each cryptocurrency has its own set of self-regulations, as well. The frequent comparison of Bitcoin to gold might lead some to believe that cryptocurrencies do not need governance because gold is not governed. But at its core, a cryptocurrency is a software project involving people and not an inanimate object. Each cryptocurrency has a team who constantly makes decisions about the project: which exchange should we list it on? How much cryptocurrency should miners be rewarded? Should we change the underlying code?

As such, cryptocurrency projects must be governed. As with governing a nation, there are various forms of governance that can be utilized for managing cryptocurrency projects. Some cryptocurrencies operate like an oligarchy with the founders or a small group of influencers having the final say on all decisions. Other cryptocurrencies are more democratic and allow those who own the coin to vote on decisions. In any company or community, strong and competent governance is necessary for success. Bad decisions and power struggles can lead to a crisis. The same holds true for cryptocurrency. When investing in a cryptocurrency, it's worth considering how it's governed. "This aspect of blockchain . . . is perhaps the greatest predictor of a particular chain's success or failure," states Investopedia.[9]

Future regulations

More regulations in the near future seem likely. As Microsoft president Brad Smith observed, "If you create technology that changes the world, the world is going to want to govern you; it's going to want in some measure to regulate you."[10] That appears to be the case with cryptocurrencies, which face a "regulatory reckoning," according to *Bitcoin Magazine*. "Things have already begun to heat up as countries around the world grapple with cryptocurrencies and try to determine how they are going to treat them."[11]

Cryptocurrencies are so new that they do not fit neatly into existing laws and governments are now just starting to adopt explicit laws. About a dozen nations, including China, Vietnam and Pakistan, have effectively banned cryptocurrency while some others, such as Malta, Bermuda and Gibraltar have enacted crypto-friendly policies aimed at appealing to blockchain companies. Overall, it remains in a legal gray area for much of the world. But as more retail and institutional investors enter the market, lawmakers worldwide are focusing more attention on cryptocurrency.

Stricter regulation of cryptocurrency is expected in the near future.

Consider the situation in America, for example, where there were 17 congressional hearings on the topic in 2017 compared to three in 2013. At a U.S. Senate hearing in February 2018, government officials announced the United States would not crack down on cryptocurrencies but instead put forth a "do no harm" approach. CFTC Chairman J. Christopher Giancarlo testified: "'Do no harm' was unquestionably the right approach to development of the Internet. Similarly, I believe that 'do no harm' is the right overarching approach for distributed ledger [blockchain] technology."[12] But Giancarlo added that U.S. officials were not completely backing away from regulation and a regulatory approach was in the works. Just one month later, the SEC announced that ICOs and exchanges operating in America must register with the SEC and comply by their strict regulations.

While the market responded with a cheer to the initial hands-off announcement, it dropped by almost 10% following the SEC's subsequent crackdown. This was no surprise given that the old guard in cryptoland fears regulation. After all, cryptocurrency was created to rebel against the government. Only 30% of Bitcoin owners said "government [should] play a stronger role in regulating Bitcoin and virtual currencies," according to a December 2017 survey by LendEDU.[13] The Bitcoin Foundation, the oldest and largest Bitcoin advocacy organization, has warned that more regulation could "stifle the adoption and use of so-called 'virtual currencies' such as Bitcoin."[14]

On the other hand, more regulation may do just the opposite. A June 2018 survey by Ipsos found that 25% of Europeans, 21% of Americans and 15% of Australians want to own cryptocurrency in the future, but right now, they think it's more risky than traditional investments.[15] The constant parade of media headlines about cryptocurrency scams and hacks certainly cannot inspire investor confidence. Institutional investors, including renowned investment firm BlackRock and major banks such as Goldman Sachs, are also eyeing cryptocurrency. But they have been hanging back due to legal uncertainties. As the *Harvard Business Review* observed in a July 2018 article, "without clear and coherent guidelines to attract good actors to the U.S. market, fraudsters might push out the good actors."[16] Indeed, cybercrimes invariably send the market crashing at least as much as, if not more than, new government regulations.

Perhaps that's why most cryptocurrency executives welcome more regulation. A 2018 survey by international law firm Foley & Lardner LLP found that 72% feel there is much legal uncertainty and 68% support government oversight of cryptocurrency trades. "There are plenty of ways to work with regulators and legislatures to develop common sense cryptocurrency laws and regulations," one executive said.[17]

Although regulations are often viewed as restrictive, they can also open up opportunities. For example, if U.S. authorities allow Bitcoin to be included in exchange-traded funds, a collection of assets that can be traded on stock exchanges, many executives surveyed believe the cryptocurrency market could experience an unprecedented boom. On the other hand, *Time* financial writer Ryan Derousseau warned that ETFs for Bitcoin might be a case of "be careful what you wish for," noting that "history is replete with examples of 'hot' investing trends turning cold once they reach sufficient popularity for the financial services industry to launch mass-marketed funds."[18]

While cryptocurrency enthusiasts debate the pros and cons, the only thing that seems certain about regulations, according to *Bitcoin Magazine*, is "that there will be some [more] soon."[19]

Notes

1 Sherwin Dowlat, "ICO Quality: Development & Trading," *Satis Group* (Mar. 21, 2018), available at https://medium.com/satis-group/ico-quality-development-trading-e4fef28df04f.
2 N.A., "Statement on Potentially Unlawful Online Platforms for Trading Digital Assets," *U.S. Securities and Exchange Commission* (Mar. 7, 2018), available at www.sec.gov/news/public-statement/enforcement-tm-statement-potentially-unlawful-online-platforms-trading.
3 N.A., "2017 Norton Cyber Security Insights Report," *Norton* (2017), available at https://us.norton.com/cyber-security-insights-2017.
4 Steven Russolillo and Eun-Young Jeong, "Cryptocurrency Exchanges Are Getting Hacked Because It's Easy," *Wall Street Journal* (July 16, 2018), available at www.wsj.com/articles/why-cryptocurrency-exchange-hacks-keep-happening-1531656000.
5 Jason Bloomberg, "Using Bitcoin or Other Cryptocurrency to Commit Crimes? Law Enforcement Is Onto You," *Forbes* (Dec. 28, 2017), available at www.forbes.com/sites/jasonbloomberg/2017/12/28/using-bitcoin-or-other-cryptocurrency-to-commit-crimes-law-enforcement-is-onto-you/.
6 Yaya J. Fanusie and Tom Robinson, "Bitcoin Laundering: An Analysis of Illicit Flows into Digital Currency Services," *Foundation for Defense of Democracies* (Jan. 12, 2018), available at http://defenddemocracy.org/content/uploads/documents/MEMO_Bitcoin_Laundering.pdf.
7 Christine Kim, "U.S. Congressman Calls for Ban on Crypto Buying and Mining," *CoinDesk* (July 18, 2018), available at www.coindesk.com/u-s-congressman-calls-for-national-ban-on-crypto-ownership/.
8 Allen Scott, "'Centralized Exchanges Are Cancer': Coinbase Shuts Gab Social Network's Account," *Bitcoinist* (June 15, 2018), available at https://bitcoinist.com/centralized-crypto-coinbase-shuts-gab/.

9 Nathan Reiff, "Governance: Blockchain Tech's Greatest Problem," *Investopedia* (July 18, 2018), available at www.investopedia.com/investing/governance-blockchain-techs-greatest-problem/.

10 David Cowan, "Cryptocurrency Regulation becomes a Top Priority," *Raconteur* (June 25, 2018), available at www.raconteur.net/finance/cryptocurrency-regulation-top-priority.

11 Andrew Nelson, "Cryptocurrency Regulation in 2018: Where the World Stands Right Now," *Bitcoin Magazine* (Feb. 1, 2018), available at https://bitcoinmagazine.com/articles/cryptocurrency-regulation-2018-where-world-stands-right-now/.

12 J. Christopher Giancarlo, "Written Testimony of Chairman J. Christopher Giancarlo before the Senate Banking Committee," *U.S. Commodities Futures Trading Commission* (Feb. 6, 2018), available at www.cftc.gov/PressRoom/SpeechesTestimony/opagiancarlo37.

13 Mike Brown, "Bitcoin Investor Sentiment Heading into 2018 | Survey & Report," *LendEDU* (Dec. 13, 2017), available at https://lendedu.com/blog/bitcoin-investor-sentiment-2018.

14 Matt Nixon, "Bitcoin Foundation Seeks Legal Protection from U.S. Currency Regulation," *Independent* (Aug. 30, 2017), available at www.independent.co.uk/news/business/news/bitcoin-foundation-legal-protection-us-currency-regulation-llew-claasen-cryptocurrency-bitlicence-a7919401.html.

15 Ipsos, "ING International Survey Mobile Banking: Cryptocurrency," *ING* (June 2018), available at https://think.ing.com/uploads/reports/ING_International_Survey_Mobile_Banking_2018.pdf.

16 Stephen J. Obie and Mark W. Rasmussen, "How Regulation Could Help Cryptocurrencies Grow," *Harvard Business Review* (July 17, 2018), available at https://hbr.org/2018/07/how-regulation-could-help-cryptocurrencies-grow.

17 Allison Charney, Patrick D. Daugherty, et al., "2018 Cryptocurrency Survey," *Foley & Lardner* (June 26, 2018), available at www.foley.com/files/uploads/Foley-Cryptocurrency-Survey.pdf.

18 Ryan Derousseau, "This Is the Clearest Sign Yet That the Bitcoin Bubble Has Burst," *Time* (Apr. 4, 2018), available at http://time.com/money/5227160/this-is-the-clearest-sign-yet-that-the-bitcoin-bubble-may-have-burst/.

19 See supra note 11 (Nelson).

7 Other topics

There are some topics that don't neatly fit into the sections we've covered but are useful to know. In this chapter, you'll learn about spending cryptocurrency, investing in initial coin offerings (or ICOs), women in blockchain, Bitcoin's relation to hate groups and human rights, psychological risks of investing and how to preserve mental well-being, cryptocurrency jobs and internships, cryptocurrency in higher education and how to stay informed about new developments in the blockchain industry.

Cryptocurrency forks

Cryptocurrencies such as Bitcoin are, at their core, software programs. As with all types of software, such as Microsoft's Windows or Apple's iOS, updates are necessary from time to time to fix weaknesses. When Bitcoin's software is updated, it's known as a *soft fork* and generally only miners need to be concerned about these changes.

However, sometimes Bitcoin's community disagrees over what changes should be made to the software. This can result in a *hard fork*. Bitcoin continues to operate as it did, but unhappy dissidents might rebel by implementing their preferred software changes on a new blockchain. This results in the creation of a new cryptocurrency. Because this new coin is based on Bitcoin's code, Bitcoin holders typically receive it for free. The amount of the new coins they receive is proportional to the amount of Bitcoins they own.

Bitcoin Cash, Bitcoin Gold and Super Bitcoin are just a few of the many hard forks that have come out of Bitcoin (also sometimes referred to as Bitcoin Core or Bitcoin Legacy to distinguish it from all the coins that now share the Bitcoin name). Besides Bitcoin, other cryptocurrencies have undergone hard forks, as well. It's important to keep up with cryptocurrency news because, if a cryptocurrency you own hard forks, you may need to move your coin to a certain wallet or exchange to ensure you receive the new coin. Binance has traditionally supported the hard forks of all cryptocurrencies listed on its exchange.

Investing in ICOs

As we covered earlier in this book, it's best to avoid investing in initial coin offerings or ICOs. For one thing, it's simply not an option for many people given government regulations. Second, it's highly risky. While some ICOs have been ridiculously successful, they are the exception. Studies show that 81% of ICOs launched since 2017 have turned out to be scams.[1]

Still, I realize some readers may have the opportunity and risk aversion necessary to invest in an ICO, if not now then perhaps down the road. If so, here are some tips:

Find ICOs: Sites such as ICO Drops and ICO Alert provide info about upcoming ICOs. They rate ICOs based on hype and interest, which saves time. They even tell you if the ICO is available in all countries.

Read their white paper: Read the white paper and evaluate the feasibility of the use case that the ICO team is claiming. Good projects will usually be easy to explain and understand. The white paper may be the most important element in an ICO. It should be well-written and provide details about the project, including the idea behind it, technology driving it, distribution of tokens and how it will be adopted and utilized. Unfortunately, many white papers don't meet these criteria. A December 2017 study by the University of Luxembourg found that a startling number of white papers lacked critical information about the projects that they represented: 18% of white papers did not contain "any information about the issuing entity"; 70% did not include any relevant legal information; 4% did not contain any information about the technology of the coin that they were representing.[2] If a company offers an ICO with scant details or doesn't provide a white paper at all, you should be suspicious.

Examine token supply: Find out how many tokens are available for presale and how many tokens the team keeps for themselves. The greater number circulating, the less unique they become due to basic supply and demand principles. This results in little or no gain for ICO investors when the cryptocurrency begins trading on exchanges. So, be wary of participating in ICOs with no cap. On the other hand, you don't want to be the only one investing in the project. Exchanges have much less interest in cryptocurrencies from projects that raised very little during their ICOs, which makes it harder to sell their tokens after release.

Background check the team: Most legitimate companies offering an ICO have no problem with providing potential investors with information about their staff. You can then verify each of the team members exists via Google searches and also try to find relevant information on social media such as LinkedIn, Twitter and Facebook along with forums such as Bitcointalk and Reddit. You should also look at their skills and experience and what their past records say about them. You need to do so in order to determine whether they have a questionable history or whether they have what it takes to see the project through.

Utilize social media: You can join an ICO's various social media channels like Reddit and Telegram to interact with the teams and assess whether the project is worth considering or just a money-making scheme for them. Is the team proactive and interested? How frequently do they communicate with their potential investors? Do they display accountability, or do they dodge your questions? If they ban you from asking questions, it's almost certainly a scam ICO. A company should provide potential investors with answers to their questions about the project. You should only invest in the ICO if you're satisfied with the answers they provide.

Avoid being scammed: In addition to the strong possibility that the ICO itself may be a scam, sometimes other scammers and hackers attempt to piggyback onto the scheme. For example, sometimes on Telegram channels, scammers try to appear as admins or company representatives and lure you into sending coins to the wrong address. Some create admin-like posts on discussion boards such as Reddit in hopes that someone will get confused and send their funds to the wrong address.

Final advice: Remember, investing in ICOs is highly risky. Never invest an amount that you cannot afford to lose.

Spending cryptocurrency

Although cryptocurrency is often purchased as a long-term investment, it can also be used as a medium for purchasing products and services.

> Cryptocurrency can be used to purchase everything from pizza to flights.

To spend your coins, you can either download a mobile app (for instance, Coinbase offers one) or sign up for a cryptocurrency debit card. Either option will circumvent the unwieldy steps necessary to convert cryptocurrency to fiat and allow you to spend your coins freely. You can buy a range of goods using cryptocurrency. One of the benefits of paying with cryptocurrency is that you don't need to give up as much personal information. You typically only need to give your name and address if you're purchasing something you want delivered.

Using cryptocurrency, you can buy flights and hotels through Expedia and CheapAir. You can buy furniture, electronics, appliances, jewelry and more on Overstock.com. If you're hungry, PizzaforCoins.com will get a pizza delivered to you in exchange for Bitcoin. If you're starving for knowledge, several universities and a few Manhattan preschools accept Bitcoin and Ethereum. For a list of stores near you that accept Bitcoin, check out SpendBitcoins.com or CoinMap.org. You can also filter your Yelp search for places that accept Bitcoin. Keep in mind, transaction costs on cryptocurrency purchases can sometimes run much higher than credit and debit cards, so it may not be worth using Bitcoin to buy small items.

Prefer to pay in cash? CoinATMradar.com lists cryptocurrency ATM locations worldwide.

Although the amount of merchant sales using cryptocurrency has increased significantly over the years – from $10 million per month in 2013 to $200 million in 2017, according to Chainalysis[3] – cryptocurrency is still not readily used by most merchants because the technology is in its early stages (Figure 7.1).

Figure 7.1 Thousands of merchants accept cryptocurrency, such as this bar in Phuket, Thailand

Source: Donovan Dirker @donovansa

Women in blockchain

Cryptocurrency has a reputation for being a male-dominated, "blockchain bro" culture, the *New York Times* reports.[4] But there are many women who have made inroads and are playing an important role in its development.

Here are some notable pioneers:

- At IBM, which is a major player in blockchain, "women run the show, from the general manager of blockchain Marie Wieck to her boss Bridget van Kralingen, to CEO Ginni Rometty," according to *Barron's*.[5]
- Kathleen Breitman is the co-founder and CEO of Tezos and developed most of the blockchain's protocol. After a highly successful ICO that raised $235 million, the cryptocurrency project hit exchanges this year and now ranks among the top-20 coins in the market.
- Elaine Shi is a leading blockchain professor at Cornell University and has developed her own cryptocurrency. She believes her cryptocurrency, Thunderchain, may be able to achieve speeds 1,000× greater than available technologies today. The project is still in its infancy, but if Thunder Token successfully develops out its product, it will revolutionize high-speed blockchains.

Because the industry is fairly nascent, it has the ability to change quickly and become much more inclusive than other fields. In many localities, there are groups women can join if they're interested in networking and learning more about cryptocurrency.

"Women, consider crypto," venture capitalist Alexia Bonatsos wrote on Twitter. "Otherwise the men are going to get all the wealth, again."[6]

Bitcoin, hate groups and human rights

Cryptocurrency often receives a lot of negative media coverage. Besides its association with criminals, it's also been associated with hate groups. The Southern Poverty Law Center says Bitcoin is the currency of choice for the "alt-right." ISIS is also reportedly heavily invested in cryptocurrency. However, cryptocurrency is also being utilized to do much good in the world.

For example, Roya Mahboob has used Bitcoin to improve women's rights in Afghanistan. The young female entrepreneur launched a company, Women's Annex, which enabled women to write blogs and make money via advertising. However, the start-up ran into problems paying contributors because none of them had bank accounts. So, Mahboob paid them instead in Bitcoin, *Forbes* reported.[7] She said one contributor whose husband beat her and confiscated her money was able to build wealth once she began earning cryptocurrency. Because her husband could no longer take her earnings, she eventually saved enough to file for divorce. Mahboob recently launched a new initiative, Digital Citizen Fund, that teaches girls about blockchain, crypto, how to code and financial literacy. *Time* named her one of the 100 most influential people in the world.

Cryptocurrency and blockchain are being used to improve human rights worldwide in many other ways, Invest in Blockchain reports. Examples include the United Nations using cryptocurrency to aid over 10,000 Syrian refugees, making money transfers more affordable in the developing world, ensuring food is being sourced ethically and without slave labor and eradicating the so-called blood diamond trade.

CoinCentral states that blockchain-related "human rights projects are growing by the day" and that "more and more blockchain and human rights use cases will develop over time."[8]

Psychological risks of investing

All that glitters is not gold, and for too many people, that includes so-called digital gold. Although cryptocurrency made some fortunes, it's left many others broken, in debt and divorced. Some investors have even committed suicide over Bitcoin. Psychiatrists have coined the term "Bitcoin Blues" to describe the widespread emotional and psychological problems that resulted from the 2018 market recession.

> Cryptocurrency is like gambling or drugs – it can become very addictive and turn into an unhealthy obsession.

Of course, these problems aren't unique to cryptocurrency. They can result from any kind of financial failure. But for many 20- and 30-somethings, cryptocurrency was their first foray into investing, and some got in over their heads.

Internet message boards are full of stories about people who had their lives wrecked by cryptocurrency investing, such as the 24-year-old Redditor who went $84,000 in debt chasing lost cryptocurrency profits.[9]

Countries such as South Korea, where 30% of people invested in cryptocurrency, were particularly hit hard by the market downturn. Tech blog Hackernoon reports,

> A lot of them had pledged their homes to buy cryptocurrency and now had to sell it for losses. Families were broken and often lead to divorces.

This led to a surge in the number of suicides reported due to losses in cryptocurrency investments. There was an increase in the number of patients visiting psychiatrist, the trauma was termed "Bitcoin Blues."[10]

You might be wondering, why didn't these idiots just sell their cryptocurrency when the market started to decline? That's easier said than done for some people. Cryptocurrency is sometimes likened to gambling or drugs – and for good reason. It can become very addictive and turn into an unhealthy obsession that toys with people's emotions and robs them of their ability to behave rationally.

As one trader described on a cryptocurrency message board,

> When a coin is going up, it can be the most euphoric experience in the world. It's unimaginable to someone from the outside. The coin becomes the best thing to ever happen to you, and you love it. Everything about it – the idea, the team, the roadmap – is perfect and can do no wrong. You are intoxicated by every spurt of growth. You fantasize about the unrealistic heights it'll achieve, setting wild benchmarks in your own imagination. You stare at the charts all day and weep with joy. You cheer on your beloved coin with all the other fans in the community, becoming an echo chamber of hype and delusion.[11]

Many an inexperienced trader experienced such feelings in 2017. They became emotionally attached to their coins. And it became impossible for them to sell when the market began to decline in 2018.

Instead, they just stared at their rising balance, awestruck by waves of euphoria and celebrating prematurely with their comrades in wealth. After the price peaked, they were in momentary disbelief that the price started going down. "It's a temporary dip," they told themselves, still suffuse with warm feelings and love for their coins. The price continued to drop; the buzz started to fade. "What's going on?" they may have wondered. They entertained for a moment the thought that maybe they should sell but didn't pull the trigger. "It's already down SO MUCH compared to the peak," they told themselves, "and surely it'll go back up. Shaking out weak hands is good after all."

After a few weeks, the price still had not gone back up. The community had largely disbanded or was wallowing in despair. The volume had dropped to almost nothing, and the price had slid steadily downward into oblivion, each day dropping to new lows that they had previously never countenanced. They were bruised and traumatized and faced with shamefully selling everything for a 95% loss.

Some investors were unable to deal with their tremendous losses, and it took a toll on their personal lives.

That's why it's important that you take steps not to end up like that.

Don't overexpose yourself financially. Don't take out loans or rack up credit card debt to buy cryptocurrency. Invest only what you can afford to lose. Don't put all of your disposable money into cryptocurrency. Be sure to diversify and invest the majority of your money in safer, traditional investments. And if you find yourself stressing over cryptocurrency, get out of it or at least talk to a professional counselor – it's not worth risking your life over.

How do you know if you've gotten yourself in too deep? Paul Merriman, a wealth management expert, recommends asking yourself three questions: "1) Have you lost sleep over an investment? 2) Do you constantly, compulsively follow the financial news over an investment? 3) Does watching financial news make you worry about your future? If you answer yes to even one of those questions, you probably have taken on too much risk," he writes.[12]

Cryptocurrency jobs and internships

Cryptocurrency and blockchain aren't just a hobby. For a growing number of people, it's a career. Despite cryptocurrency's current bear market, jobs in the industry are booming. Glassdoor, a popular jobs website, recently released a report that found cryptocurrency jobs in America increased by 300% in the past year.[13]

Most of the industry's job openings are tech related, of course, but there are also plenty of jobs available for those who are interested in cryptocurrency but lack the coding and computer skills. For anyone looking to enter the cryptocurrency space, programming skills are helpful. Glassdoor's report shows that 55% of blockchain jobs are either for engineering or tech-related work, with software engineering alone accounted for 19% of job postings. With demand for employees up, so are salaries. The average earnings of a blockchain engineer have soared to between $150,000 and $175,000 per year, according to Hired's 2018 State of Salaries Report.[14] That's much higher than the $135,000 average software engineer salary.

But if you're not a techie, don't worry. A significant number of non-technical roles have become prominent. This phenomenon is not unique to blockchain: Glassdoor has previously found that tech companies begin to offer nontechnical positions as they grow. Non-tech roles include various management roles such as product managers, along with crypto-specific positions in accounting, PR/marketing, journalism and more – all of which do not require IT acumen. And, of course, some cryptocurrency investors have quit their day jobs in other fields to work full time as day traders.

New York City and San Francisco offer the most job opportunities in the U.S. cryptocurrency industry, accounting for 24% and 21% of all job openings, respectively. Outside of America, London, Singapore, Toronto and Hong Kong have the most job openings. If you're looking to break into the industry, the best thing to do is begin with an internship.

Internships and jobs can be found online via job search sites, such as indeed.com, LinkedIn and CryptocurrencyJobs. Networking through local conferences and events, MeetUp.com events and alumni connections can also lead to jobs. Keep in mind that in cryptocurrency, like most industries, many jobs are never officially advertised, so who you know matters.

Cryptocurrency education

Interest in cryptocurrency is booming on college campuses, the *New York Times*[15] and *Fortune*[16] report.

A recent Coinbase study found that about 40% of the world's top-50 universities offer at least one undergraduate course in cryptocurrencies or blockchain.[17] In September 2018, New York University announced the launch of a new major in blockchain technology – the first program of its kind in the United States. Meanwhile, many schools, such as City University of New York–Baruch, have created crypto clubs that are quite active, regularly hosting public events and making blog posts.

University students' interest in blockchain is also evident from a study by Student Loan Report, which found that 21% of students had used some of their loan money to invest in cryptocurrency.[18] Colleges are investing in cryptocurrency, as well. Yale University, for example, recently invested part of its endowment in cryptocurrency.

How academia can help cryptocurrency

Higher education's interest in cryptocurrency and blockchain is beneficial for the industry for a couple big reasons. First, there's a growing demand for employees who have experience and training in this field. Second, academia could help fix some of the fraud that's prevalent in the market.

Your education shouldn't end with this book. Many inexpensive and free resources are readily available online.

As tech blog Finance Magnates explains,

> At the moment, peer-reviewed whitepapers and blockchain papers are certainly out there, but they are far more likely to be the exception than the rule. While some of these unreviewed platforms and whitepapers may attribute their lack of scientific accountability to the scarcity of possibilities to get a white paper peer-reviewed, there are a large number of platforms that take advantage as the lack of accountability within the space as an opportunity to swindle unsuspecting consumers. However, the presence of an established academic community in the blockchain industry could attribute to an expectation of higher accountability standards. In other words, even if peer-review isn't an enforced requirement, it could be something that consumers and users come to expect.[19]

Staying informed

If you enjoyed this book and want to be involved with blockchain and cryptocurrency in the future (either as an investor or as a career), it's important to continue your education. There are many other ways to learn:

- Cornell, Oxford and other top universities offer six- to eight-week online certificate programs on blockchain, but they cost money.
- If you're looking for a less expensive option, Udemy.com offers a variety of cryptocurrency and blockchain-related short online courses for about $20 per course. Lynda.com also offers some basic, affordable courses on these topics.
- Princeton University offers a free online course and textbook on cryptocurrency, although it's much more technical than this book and geared toward computer science students.
- There are countless books by experts sold on Amazon (although some are better than others, so check out reviews).

Additionally, you should regularly read cryptocurrency news sites. Again, some sources are better than others. A recent investigative report by blockchain blog Breaker found that more than half of the popular cryptocurrency news sites are pay-for-play, meaning they provide coverage in exchange for money.[20] Essentially, they're accepting bribes for positive news stories, which means they are not really unbiased, objective and independent as good journalists should be. Therefore, their coverage can't be relied on for accuracy.

Not all news sites are sketchy, though. Here are some crypto news sites that seem good:

- CoinDesk
- CCN

- *Bitcoin Magazine*
- The Block
- CryptoSlate
- Messari

And here are some good academic journals available free online:

- *Ledger Journal*
- *Stanford Journal of Blockchain Law & Policy*

Your education shouldn't end with this book. Strive to be a lifelong learner. Blockchain and cryptocurrency are rapidly evolving. Many inexpensive and free resources are readily available online, so there's no excuse for not staying informed.

Notes

1 Sherwin Dowlat, "ICO Quality: Development & Trading," *Satis Group* (Mar. 21, 2018), available at https://medium.com/satis-group/ico-quality-development-trading-e4fef28df04f.

2 Rachel McIntosh, "Study Reveals Critical Information Is Missing from ICO Whitepapers," *Finance Magnates* (June 12, 2017), available at www.financemagnates.com/cryptocurrency/news/study-reveals-critical-information-missing-ico-whitepapers/.

3 Annie Nova, "Bitcoin Takes on Cash, as More Places Accept the Cryptocurrency," *CNBC* (Mar. 2, 2018), available at www.cnbc.com/2018/03/02/spending-cryptocurrencies-on-everyday-purchases-is-getting-easier.html.

4 Nellie Bowles, "Women in Cryptocurrencies Push Back against 'Blockchain Bros'," *New York Times* (Feb. 25, 2018), available at www.nytimes.com/2018/02/25/business/cryptocurrency-women-blockchain-bros.html.

5 Avi Saltzman, "4 Women Who Make a Difference in Blockchain," *Barron's* (Aug. 20, 2018), available at www.barrons.com/articles/4-women-who-make-a-difference-in-blockchain-1534554704.

6 Alexia Bonatsos, tweet via @alexia account, *Twitter* (Jan. 25, 2018), available at https://twitter.com/alexia/status/956569295017906176.

7 Laura Shin, "How Bitcoin Solved This Serial Entrepreneur's Problems," *Forbes* (Aug. 8, 2017), available at www.forbes.com/sites/laurashin/2017/08/08/how-bitcoin-solved-this-serial-entrepreneurs-problems/#500d33df309c.

8 Christina Comben, "How Blockchain Is Being Applied to Human Rights," *CoinCentral* (Sept. 5, 2018), available at https://coincentral.com/blockchain-and-human-rights/.

9 FinanciallyFacked, "Please Learn from My Mistake(s) . . . How I've Financially Ruined Everything in Less Than 12 Months," *Reddit* (Sept. 12, 2018), available at www.reddit.com/r/Buttcoin/comments/9fe7cz/rpersonalfinance_user_learns_the_hard_way_that/e5w99jz/.

10 CoinSwitch, "Inside Korea's Cryptocurrency Drama: Suicide, Divorces and Broken Hopes," *Hackernoon* (May 19, 2018), available at https://hackernoon.

com/inside-koreas-cryptocurrency-drama-suicide-divorces-and-broken-hopes-67866e26145f.

11 Deranged Tinder Pumo, "Here's Why It's Impossible to Make Money in Crypto (I Lost 95%)," *AutoAdmit* (Aug. 4, 2018), available at http://xoxohth.com/thread.php?thread_id=4042486&mc=17&forum_id=2.

12 Paul A. Merriman, "The Emotional and Psychological Risks of Investing," *MarketWatch* (Mar. 30, 2016), available at www.marketwatch.com/story/the-emotional-and-psychological-risks-of-investing-2016-03-30.

13 Daniel Zhou, "The Rise of Bitcoin & Blockchain: A Growing Demand for Talent," *Glassdoor* (Oct. 18, 2018), available at www.glassdoor.com/research/rise-in-bitcoin-jobs/.

14 Macy Bayern, "Salaries for Blockchain Engineers Are Soaring as Demand for Expertise Explodes," *TechRepublic* (Oct. 23, 2018), available at www.techre public.com/article/salaries-for-blockchain-engineers-are-soaring-as-demand-for-expertise-explodes/.

15 Nathaniel Popper, "Cryptocurrencies Come to Campus," *New York Times* (Feb. 18, 2018), available at www.nytimes.com/2018/02/08/technology/cryptocurren cies-come-to-campus.html.

16 Jeff John Roberts, "The Hot New Subject on Campus? It's Blockchain," *Fortune* (Aug. 28, 2018), available at http://fortune.com/2018/08/28/blockchain-courses/.

17 N.A., "The Rise of Crypto in Higher Education," *Coinbase* (Aug. 28, 2018), available at https://blog.coinbase.com/the-rise-of-crypto-in-higher-education-81b648c2466f.

18 Greg Toppo, "For Students in Debt, Bitcoin on Their Minds," *Inside Higher Ed* (Apr. 12, 2018), available at www.insidehighered.com/news/2018/04/12/sur vey-1-5-college-students-loans-used-aid-buy-bitcoin-or-other-cryptocurrencies.

19 Rachel McIntosh, "Behind the Scenes: How Academia Is Shaping the Future of Crypto," *Finance Magnates* (Sept. 27, 2018), available at www.finance magnates.com/cryptocurrency/news/behind-the-scenes-how-academia-is-shaping-the-future-of-crypto/.

20 Corine Faife, "We Asked Crypto News Outlets If They'd Take Money to Cover a Project: More Than Half Said Yes," *Breaker* (Oct. 25, 2018), available at https://breakermag.com/we-asked-crypto-news-outlets-if-theyd-take-money-to-cover-a-project-more-than-half-said-yes/.

8 Resources

This book has a companion website, CryptocurrencyTextbook.com, which provides additional information, including instructional videos and useful links. Additionally, the following are some other helpful online resources for cryptocurrency.

Check out this book's companion website at Cryptocurrency Textbook.com.

- **Bitcoin.org**: A primer on everything you want to know about Bitcoin, including a copy of Satoshi Nakamoto's white paper.
- **CryptocurrencyFacts.com**: Simple explanations on what cryptocurrency is and how it works.
- **BlockGeeks.com**: Educational articles and videos to help you understand cryptocurrency and blockchain.
- **Udemy.com**: Offers several video courses for about $20 that explain cryptocurrency and blockchain.
- **CoinMarketGame.com**: Practice trading cryptocurrency using this free online mock cryptocurrency exchange.
- **CryptoCasey.com**: Step-by-step videos on how to buy Bitcoin, Ethereum and alternative coins.
- **Coinbase.com**: Secure, easy-to-use and regulated U.S. exchange that's good for making your initial cryptocurrency investments.
- **Binance.com**: International cryptocurrency exchange with a good reputation that sells many cryptocurrencies.
- **Blockfolio.com**: Free app that can be downloaded to your smartphone to monitor your cryptocurrency portfolio.
- **CoinMarketCap.com**: Ranks and provides info about cryptocurrencies, such as marketcap, coin supply, price and exchanges.

- **MarketBeat.com** and **CoinPaprika.com**: Similar to CoinMarketCap, but they provide even more info about cryptocurrencies.
- **Messari.io**: Research and FA on various cryptocurrencies.
- **CCN.com**, **CoinDesk.com** and **TheBlockCrypto.com**: Get the latest news on cryptocurrency.
- **Bitcointalk.org**: Popular online discussion forum about cryptocurrency.
- **Coindar.org**: A cryptocurrency events calendar with updates on when coins will be listed on new exchanges, hard forks, new products, etc.
- **Alternative.me**: Its "Crypto Fear & Greed Index" tool analyzes a variety of sources to gauge the current sentiment of the Bitcoin market.
- **DeadCoins.com**: A frequently updated list of cryptocurrency projects that have been abandoned and, therefore, should not be invested in.
- **ICO Drops**: Provides info about upcoming ICOs.
- **CryptocurrencyJobs.co**: Find cryptocurrency and blockchain job listings.
- **CoinATMradar.com**: Lists cryptocurrency ATM locations, where you can purchase cryptocurrency with fiat or cash out cryptocurrency.
- **SpendBitcoins.com** and **CoinMap.org**: Lists merchants that accept cryptocurrency as payment.

Glossary

Hodl, vaporware, dead cat bounce. Cryptocurrency has it has its own dialect filled with computing, financial and legal jargons – some of which are downright bizarre – making it a daunting challenge to learn the ropes. The following are some of the most common terms used.

Abandonware   A cryptocurrency project that has been abandoned by its founders/owner and is no longer being developed or supported.

Airdrop   When a blockchain company distributes cryptocurrency tokens to the wallets of some users free of charge. This is typically done to help promote the token.

Altcoin   Short for "alternative coin," it's generally any cryptocurrency other than Bitcoin or Ethereum (though some Bitcoin enthusiasts consider Ethereum an altcoin).

ATH   An acronym for "all-time high," it refers to the highest price that a particular cryptocurrency has ever achieved.

ATL   An acronym for "all-time low," it refers to the lowest price that a particular cryptocurrency has ever achieved.

Bagholder   Someone still holding a cryptocurrency with sinking value and bad future prospects or following a pump-and-dump crash.

Bear/bearish   Negative sentiment or downward price movement for a particular coin or the general market.

Bear trap   A figurative trap where a general upward price trend reverses downward momentarily but will resume its upward motion.

Block   A group of transactions linked together on the blockchain.

Blockchain   A ledger showing every single record of transactions in order, dating back to the very first one.

Block reward   Payment given to miners to incentivize them to process transactions on a decentralized blockchain network such as Bitcoin.

BTD   Acronym for "buy the dip," it's an indication to buy a coin when it has significantly decreased in price and is expected to rebound.

Bull/bullish   Positive sentiment or upward price movement for a particular coin or the general market.

Bull trap   A figurative trap where a general decreasing price movement reverses upward momentarily but will resume its downward motion.

Byzantine fault tolerance   An algorithm used to settle disputes among network participants and achieve consensus on confirming transactions for the blockchain.

Centralized/centralization   When a single entity has control of all records in its ledger, it is considered to be centralized. This is how banks operate.

CFTC   Stands for U.S. Commodity Futures Trading Commission, one of the primary U.S. government agencies involved in the regulation of cryptocurrency in America.

CMC   Stands for CoinMarketCap, a free website that lists marketcap rankings, charts and other information for all cryptocurrencies being sold on exchanges.

Coin burn   This occurs when a cryptocurrency's team reduces its coin supply in order to make it rarer and thus hopefully raise its value.

Cold storage   Storing the private keys for your cryptocurrency offline in a device or on a piece of paper.

DApp   Acronym for "decentralized application," it refers to an application that uses an Ethereum smart contract as its underlying code.

Day trading   The buying and selling of a cryptocurrency within a short trading period, usually the same day.

DCA   Acronym for "dollar cost average," it's a cryptocurrency buying strategy that involves spending the same dollar amount every certain period of time to purchase a coin rather than purchasing a coin all at once with your available funds.

Dead cat bounce   A temporary recovery in prices after a big decrease, it can mislead investors into thinking a downward trend has ceased long term.

Dead coin   Cryptocurrency coins and initial coin offering token sales that have failed, fizzled or fallen in the virtual landfill. These coins are not being actively developed.

Decentralized/decentralization   Used to describe a ledger that is not controlled by a single entity and instead shares, replicates and synchronizes its data across many computers.

Depth chart   A chart visualizing requests to buy (known as bids) and requests to sell (known as asks) on an exchange.

Double spend   Attempting to send the same coin(s) to two different places at the same time.

Dump/dumping   Selling your cryptocurrency or downward price movements due to increasing selling pressure by many others.

DYOR   Acronym for "do your own research," it means you should never buy a coin just because someone else says to or without conducting a fundamental analysis first.

ETF   Acronym for "exchange-traded funds," it's a collection of assets that can be traded on stock exchanges.

ELI5 Acronym for "explain like I'm 5," it means please provide an explanation that's so simplified that even a 5-year-old could understand.

Encryption Converting plain text into unintelligible text with the use of an algorithm.

Exchange Online platforms where you can buy and sell cryptocurrencies. Some popular U.S.-based exchanges are Coinbase and Gemini.

FA Stands for "fundamental analysis"; it involves researching a coin's white paper, purpose, team, partnerships, roadmap, room for price growth and other factors to assess its viability and potential.

Fiat Government-issued currency, such as the U.S. dollar or euro.

51% attack Occurs when a person or entity controls a majority of the computer power on a blockchain network and therefore can negatively affect a cryptocurrency by halting mining, stopping or changing transactions, and double-spending coins.

"The Flippening" A potential future event wherein Ethereum's (or some other altcoin's) marketcap surpasses Bitcoin's marketcap, dethroning Bitcoin as the most "valuable" cryptocurrency.

FOMO Acronym for "fear of missing out," it's a rookie mistake where a cryptocurrency is skyrocketing, and you think it will pump more so you buy at the peak price.

Forger Similar to miners on Proof of Work networks, these are people who use their computing power to process transactions for blockchain networks that utilize a Proof of Stake protocol.

Fork When the blockchain is split due to competing philosophies or a software upgrade. It sometimes results in a new altcoin being created.

FUD Acronym for "fear, uncertainty and doubt," it describes a time of panic where negative sentiments are exaggerated.

Futures Basically, a bet between two parties about the future price of a cryptocurrency. You can go "long," meaning you expect the price to increase, or bet that prices will fall, known as "shorting."

Gas The small fee paid to miners who process transactions on the Ethereum network.

Genesis block The first set of transactions on a blockchain.

Hardware wallet A device that can securely store cryptocurrency offline in cold storage, making it arguably the most secure way to hold cryptocurrency.

Hash The encrypted data units stored on the blockchain.

Hodl Crypto slang for "hold," it's the act of holding on to your cryptocurrency and resisting the urge to sell, even in dire market circumstances. The term is a meme that originated from a typo several years ago on a Bitcoin forum post.

House money Derived from gambling slang, it refers to one's profits from the cryptocurrency exchange ("the house"). It's the money you've made above the money you initially invested out of your own pocket.

ICO   Stands for "initial coin offering"; it's a means by which funds are raised for a new cryptocurrency venture, usually through a coin presale.

Institutional investor   A large organization, such as a bank, hedge fund or investment firm that makes substantial investments.

KYC   Acronym for "Know Your Customer." In order to prevent cryptocurrency from being used for money laundering activities, many governments require exchanges to verify a customer's identity before they can use the exchange.

Laddering   This is a cryptocurrency trading strategy that involves incrementally moving in and out of positions. Instead of buying or selling at a single price, one would set incremental buy/sell limit orders throughout an exchange's order book and buy when the price goes down or sell when the price goes up.

Lambo   Short for Lamborghini – what many cryptocurrency investors dream of buying when they become rich. Crypto traders will often jokingly ask "when lambo" on social media in reference to when will a coin moon.

Ledger Nano S/Trezor   Arguably the two most popular hardware wallet devices.

Limit order/limit buy/limit sell   Orders placed by traders to buy or sell a cryptocurrency when a certain price point is reached.

Long   Buying coins, expecting the price to increase at a certain point in the future.

Market order/market buy/market sell   A purchase or sale on an exchange at the current price. Market buys purchase the cheapest cryptocurrency available on the order book while market sells fill the most expensive buy order on the book.

MCAP   Market capitalization of a cryptocurrency, which is an indicator of its market size. It's calculated from multiplying a cryptocurrency's average exchange price by the total available supply of coins currently in the market.

MEW   Acronym for MyEtherWallet, a website that provides free "wallets" for storing cryptocurrencies.

Miner   A person who uses computing power to process transactions on a blockchain network that utilizes a Proof of Work protocol.

Mining pool   When a group of miners combine their computing power to process transactions in order to increase their chances of winning block rewards.

Moon   Significant upward movement of a cryptocurrency's price, toward the moon.

Network   Refers to all the computers used to operate a blockchain.

Node   A computer operating on a blockchain network.

P2P   Abbreviation for "peer-to-peer," it's a type of network where two or more computers exchange data with each other without a centralized third party being used as an intermediary.

Permissionless vs. permissioned blockchain   Used to describe whether a blockchain network is open to everyone to validate transactions on or restricted to certain people.

PoS   Stands for "Proof of Stake." It's a network system where individuals validate block transactions according to how many coins they hold. It's a more efficient alternative to the Proof of Work model.

PoW   Acronym for "Proof of Work." It's the original network system for blockchain used to confirm transactions and add new blocks to the chain. This system is open to everyone, including non-coin holders, and individuals compete against each other to complete transactions on the network for rewards.

Private key   The password for your wallet, consisting of a long string of letters and numbers. You need your private key when selling or withdrawing cryptocurrencies because it acts as your digital signature. You should never share your private key with anyone; otherwise, they can steal your cryptocurrency.

Public key   A unique wallet address, which appears as a long string of numbers and letters, used to send and receive cryptocurrencies. For example, Bitcoin public keys are alphanumeric strings that begin with a 1 or 3; Ethereum public keys begin with '0x.' Public keys usually require private keys to exclusively access the funds. You may share your public key with others when you want to make a transaction.

Public vs. private blockchain   Used to describe whether a blockchain ledger is publicly viewable or if its access is restricted to certain individuals. Some purists consider only publicly viewable ledgers to be bona fide blockchains.

Pump   Upward price movement.

Pump-and-dump   Used to describe altcoins that receive lots of social media attention, which leads to a fast price increase, and then is followed by a huge crash – often over and over again. Such price manipulation is often attributed to whales or collectives.

Rekt   A slang that refers to "wrecked" or suffering great losses in cryptocurrency trades.

Retail investor   An individual who invests.

Reverse indicator   Someone who is seemingly always wrong predicting a coin's or the market's price movements.

Rig   A special computer system used to mine cryptocurrency.

Roadmap   A multiyear plan that outlines a cryptocurrency project's plan to develop its product and gain users.

ROI   Stands for "return on investment." It's the percentage of how much money has been made compared to an initial investment (i.e., 100% ROI means someone doubled their money).

Satoshi   The smallest unit of Bitcoin, named after Bitcoin's mysterious founder Satoshi Nakamoto.

SEC   Stands for U.S. Securities and Exchange Commission, one of the primary U.S. government agencies that regulates cryptocurrencies in America.

Sell wall/buy wall   Using a depth chart, traders can see the current limit buy and sell points and their graphical representation looks like walls.

Sharding   A way of splitting up the full blockchain history so each node doesn't need the full copy of it. It's a scaling solution for blockchains that improves efficiency. As a blockchain grows larger, network performance slows if every node is required to carry the full blockchain.

Shilling   Promoting a particular cryptocurrency, usually shamelessly. If a coin is promised to be the next Bitcoin or provide some kind of blockchain breakthrough, it's being shilled.

Shitcoin   A coin with no use, value or potential.

Short   Selling coins, expecting the price to plunge.

Slippage   The difference between the expected price of a trade and the price at which the trade actually executes.

Software wallet   Storing cryptocurrency in software files or apps on a computer or smartphone.

Spread   The difference between the seller's price and buyer's price.

Stable coin   A cryptocurrency with extremely low volatility. Tether is an example of a stable coin, as its value always hovers around one U.S. dollar regardless of market volatility.

TA   Stands for "technical analysis." It's an analysis that attempts to predict future prices based on charts showing historical price movements and other indicators.

Team   The people who develop and manage a cryptocurrency.

Tether   A cryptocurrency token claimed by its creators to be backed by one U.S. dollar for each token issued. While this claim is often doubted because it has not been publicly audited, Tether has yet to experience any financial problems.

Vaporware   A project that is never actually developed or implemented, making it synonymous with being a shitcoin.

Volatility   The fluctuation in a cryptocurrency's price.

Whale   Someone who owns a huge amount of a particular cryptocurrency and therefore can influence its price.

White paper   A detailed written proposal by a blockchain's development team that outlines the purpose and mechanics of its cryptocurrency.

Wei   The smallest unit of Ether, the cryptocurrency of the Ethereum network. It's named in tribute to Wei Dai, a computer engineer who was influential in the development of Bitcoin.

Figure BM.1 Illustration of cryptocurrency slang in use

Source: Extra Fabulous Comics

Index

Printed in the United States
by Baker & Taylor Publisher Services